LONDON
BUSES

Kevin Lane

Contents

Introduction	3	London General Transport	
Where to Go	5	Services Ltd	64
Armchair Passenger Transport Co Ltd	8	London Sovereign	67
Arriva Croydon & North Surrey Ltd	10	London United Busways Ltd/	
Arriva East Herts & Essex Ltd	13	Stanwell Buses Ltd	68
Arriva Kent Thameside Ltd	16	Metrobus Ltd	72
Arriva London North Ltd	18	Metroline Travel Ltd	74
Arriva London North East Ltd	21	MTL London Northern Ltd	77
Arriva London South	23	Nostalgiabus Ltd	82
Arriva The Shires	26	Sovereign Buses (Harrow) Ltd	82
Capital Citybus Ltd	27	South East London & Kent Bus Co Ltd	
Capital Logistics	30	(Selkent)	83
CentreWest London Buses Ltd	31	Tellings – Golden Miller Ltd	87
Crystals Coaches	37	Thamesway	88
East London Bus & Coach Co Ltd		F. E. Thorpe	90
(Stagecoach East London)	40	Sightseeing and Other Buses	91
Epsom Buses	45	Appendix 1: Class Prefixes;	
Harris Bus Co Ltd	48	Former London Bus Companies	94
Limebourne Travel	52	Appendix 2: The Major Bus-Owning	
London Buslines	53	Groups in London	95
London Central Bus Co Ltd	56		

Front cover: Stagecoach Selkent Leyland Titan T1101 (B101 WUV) crosses London Bridge as it returns to its home garage in Catford. **Philip Lamb**

Back cover: MCW MetroRider 102 of Arriva North London is seen here returning south of the river having just crossed Waterloo Bridge. **Philip Lamb**

First published 1998

ISBN 0 7110 2596 7

Published by Ian Allan Publishing

an imprint of Ian Allan Publishing Ltd, Terminal House, Station Approach, Shepperton, Surrey TW17 8AS.

Printed by Ian Allan Printing Ltd at its works at Riverdene Business Park, Molesey Road, Hersham, Surrey KT12 4RG.

Code: 9808/C2

Introduction

must be some 20 years since the last *abc London*
uses was published by Ian Allan. That title was
ssentially only a fleetbook, whereas this is more of an
erall guide to present-day operations.
he intervening years have seen many changes,
ainly in the areas of tendering and privatisation, and
e fleet itself is, with a few notable exceptions,
recognisable from that of 1978. However, there is
me common ground to explore. That old
pendable, the Routemaster, soldiers on in 1998, 42
ars since RM1 entered service at Cricklewood in
bruary 1956 and the only class still in service from
e 1950s' abcs! Taking into account the demise of
e type on MTL route 139 in March 1998, there are
ll around 600 Routemasters in service with the
rmer London Bus units, London Sovereign and
staglabus. Add to these the various vehicles used
 sightseeing operators, and it can be seen that the
pe is far from dead in London.
wo other double-deckers which were around, albeit
ly just, in 1978 were the Leyland Titans and
etrobuses of classes T and M respectively. Both
pes are common in certain areas, although both
ve been subject to withdrawals, more so in the case
 the Titan, which was previously a model almost
clusive to London. Although they will be in service
r a long time yet, they are looking their age in
mparison to the latest offerings from DAF and Volvo.
he last class to have survived is a handful of
-class Leyland Nationals dating from 1976-9 and
erating with London United and Westlink. Except for
e Greenway conversions of 'Red Arrow' Leyland
ational 2s with London General, the type has been
moved from the London fleets, except for a few in
e as mobility buses. Not actually in service are the
rviving BL-class Bristol LHs, used as driver trainers
 CentreWest and dating from 1976/7.
So what is running in London today? In some areas it
ems that the answer is the Dennis Dart, and
hough this is said with tongue in cheek, it has
rtainly become a new London standard. It comes in
any shapes and sizes: long, short, low-floor etc, and
is sheer variety is typical of the London scene of
day. Since the days of the semi-autonomous bus
erating units of the late 1980s, and the delights of
ute tendering, small batches of vehicles have been
ught or leased for specific jobs. The days of 'start a
w route and stick a couple of RFs on it' are long
ne. If there is a new double-deck standard, then it
ust be the Volvo Olympian, although other types to
counter include older Leyland Olympians, DAF
3250s, Volvo Citybuses, Scania N113s, Dennis
ominators and Arrows…the list goes on. Other
ngle-deck types include the Dennis Lance, DAF

Optare Deltas, a few Leyland Lynxes and mini- and
midibuses. Of the latter, only Ford Transits of the FS
class were represented back in 1978.

However, amid all this vehicular progress, we also
have route tendering. The first routes were put out to
tender, with operations getting underway in July 1985.
Both London Buses and other operators could bid to
run routes, bringing a (then) welcome injection of
colour to our streets. Initial routes put out to tender
were in the suburbs and it wasn't until Grey-Green
took over on the 24 in November 1988 that
independent operation could be experienced in the
heart of London. Its grey, green and orange Volvo
Citybuses were certainly noticeable amid a sea of red!
Since then, the sight of operators other than the
former London bus companies working in central
London is quite commonplace, although the current
requirement for such buses to be at least 80% red,
does render them less conspicuous to the uninitiated
observer.

The last 13 years of route tendering has seen quite a
diversity of operators come and go, from hitherto little-
known independents to National Bus Company
subsidiaries. Such familiar and not so familiar names
to be involved in tendered services over the years
have included Atlas Bus, Boro'line Maidstone,
Cityrama, Eastern National, Frontrunner South East,
EnsignBus, R&I Tours, Scancoaches and Transcity Link
Ltd. New names to come onto the scene lately include
Capital Coaches, Capital Logistics and, due during the
summer of 1998, West Midlands Travel, trading as
Travel London.

Another major change from 20 years ago is the
disappearance of the familiar roundel from the sides
of the buses, in favour of the fleetname and logo of
the new companies. It does still appear on the slip-
boards of tendered services, alongside 'London
Transport Bus Service' and is of course prominent in
publicity.

It will be noted throughout the following pages that
the long-established practice of class-prefixes to fleet
numbers is still adhered to by the new owners of the
former London bus units, at least for the most part.
Some Selkent Darts and Olympians do not carry
prefixes, for example. It should be noted, also, that a
different prefix may now refer to the same type of
vehicle, depending on the operator.

Another point to notice is route allocation of vehicles.
In many cases this should be used as a guide only, as
in practice a different type of vehicle may come along
to that expected, but this does vary from area to area.
Some routes are a safe bet, of course; a Routemaster
will generally turn up where it should and some routes
that require specific vehicles usually retain them.

Others may simply turn out a double-decker of whatever type is available. Even the current practice of route-branding a vehicle will not necessarily ensure its use where it should! Up-to-date information can be found on a monthly basis within the pages of *Buses* magazine (published by Ian Allan), while the various publications produced by LOTS (the London Omnibus Traction Society) are very useful, as is membership of the society itself!

Thanks are due to John Aldridge, writer of the 'In London' column in *Buses*, for checking my text and, as usual, to my long-suffering wife, Maureen, for putting up with the mess caused by another book.

Above: *London General NV163 (R363 LGH), a Northern Counties Palatine II-bodied Volvo Olympian, leaves Baker Street on a route 74 service to Roehampton in March 1998.* **Kevin Lane**

Where to Go

o the occasional visitor to London, or even to those who might go more regularly, the bus scene must resent quite a bewildering array of routes and ehicles. Where then, does one begin to explore the omnibological' delights of the capital?

For complete travel freedom in London, the ideal cket is the one-day travelcard, available not only on nost buses, but also the Underground, the Docklands Light Railway and the various former British Rail companies. It can be used after 09.30 on weekdays and at any time at weekends and can be pought from underground stations, main line railway tations, London Transport information centres and some newsagents. It can also be bought outside the ravelcard area in conjunction with a railway ticket.

The travelcard area is divided into zones 1-6, priced according to where you want to go. It ranges from central zones 1 and 2, at £2.80, up to all zones at £4.30. These are the adult rates; children pay £1.80 regardless of the number of zones. Other tickets are available and there is a guide to tickets, fares and zones which is available free from ticket offices etc. As a rough guide, however, the travelcard boundary ie all zones), is Uxbridge, Harrow, Edgware, Barnet, Cockfosters, Enfield, Chingford, Epping, Romford, Upminster, Erith, Orpington, Croydon, Purley, Cheam, Surbiton, Feltham, Heathrow Airport and West Drayton. All of the underground system, with the exception of the Metropolitan Line north of Moor Park, is included. Bus journeys tend to be rather slow, so the underground network and British Rail are ideal for getting to the places of interest.

It is probable that the first-time visitor to London will want to sample a Routemaster or two. All routes, with the exception of Nostalgiabus 306, can be seen in zone 1. The current list of operators and routes are as follows: CentreWest (7, 23), Leaside (38, 73), South London (19, 137, 159), London Central (12, 36), London General (11, 14, 22), London Sovereign (13), London United (9, 94), Metroline (6, 98), MTL (10), and East London (8, 15). Their individual routes can be followed on maps available from LT Travel Centres, but all can easily be covered in a day with ease. Note, however, that these are worked by Routemasters on Mondays to Saturdays only (or Mondays to Fridays in the case of the 11) and many do not run in the evening, being replaced by one-man vehicles.

All the former red bus companies, except for Westlink, work into central London. A few choice examples include London Central's route 3, on which

Optare Spectras are used, London General with its impressive Northern Counties Palatine II-bodied Volvo Olympians on route 74, and East London's London City Airport low-floor Darts, to be seen at Liverpool Street station (please note that the LT Travelcard is not valid on this service). A number of other operators now work on tendered services in central London: Capital Citybus, Grey-Green, Limebourne Travel, London Sovereign, F. E. Thorpe and Travel London.

Before heading out into the suburbs, a word about other types of operation. The tourist trails are well served by sightseeing buses and are well worth a study in themselves. Leaflets giving details of routes, fares, etc can be picked up all over the place, including at underground stations. Indeed, there are many interesting photographs to be had of other buses from the top deck of one of the open-toppers, something I have yet to get around to doing…
Sightseeing coaches seem to be everywhere, again at all the tourist attractions. Good places to see them are Bank, Trafalgar Square, Marble Arch and the Embankment, although traffic may make them awkward to photograph in some places.

National Express services work into Victoria coach station, but since its refurbishment passengers are discouraged from getting anywhere near the vehicles themselves, being held behind glass doors until departure. Gone are the days when one could wander around with a camera and photograph whatever took your fancy, although from a safety point of view this was always a little risky. It is certainly easier and more satisfying to photograph the coaches in the surrounding streets.

On the edge of the central area one could give Aldgate a try. As well as the former red bus companies, there are Capital Citybus on the 67 and Grey-Green on the 78. Aldgate is also the terminus of several limited-stop services from out of town and is quite busy at peak periods. To the west of town, Shepherds Bush Green can be recommended for Armchair Olympians on the 237 and CentreWest's V-class Volvo Olympians on the 607, whence it is a short journey to Ealing Broadway. The area around the station is busy with buses, including Armchair Darts and Olympians, CentreWest single- and double-deckers and MTL Darts on the 112.

Heading further west, Hounslow is a worthwhile stopping-off point, with the bus station and London United garage a short walk from Hounslow East station. A good variety of vehicle types can be seen, including London United's Leyland Nationals on route H37, London & Country's Darts on the H28 and Telling-Golden Miller's Darts on the 235.

Heathrow Airport, at the end of the Piccadilly Line, is a mecca for bus and coach services, the bus station being situated away from Terminals 1, 2 and 3. Many out-of-town routes also terminate here, bringing a fair mix of 'provincial' operators. In addition, there is the constant flow of transfer and other internal workings which can include some exotic vehicle types. Hatton Cross, the stop before Heathrow, has its own little bus station and plays host to Capital Logistics on the H25, London Buslines on the 285 and 490 as well as London United route H25 and Metroline 90. Other services into the airport pass nearby, including limited-stop 726, now operated by Capital Logistics.

To the southwest, Kingston is always a rewarding place to see and photograph buses, with several busy areas. There are two bus stations: Fairfield and Cromwell Road, the latter being used more by out-of-town routes. Over the road are the Westlink garage and old bus station, dating from 1922 and 1928 respectively. The 'Smokebox' bookshop is also adjacent and worth a visit! Fairfield bus station is a few minutes' walk away, although Eden Street is a better bet, where many routes pass, including Routemaster-worked Nostalgiabus route 306.

Another area to the south worth a visit is Croydon, currently resembling a building site due to the construction of the Tramlink. Arriva Croydon & North Surrey, Capital Logistics, Metrobus, South London, Selkent and Epsom Buses will all be encountered, with more activity around West Croydon, where there is a bus station.

Several parts of east London come to mind as good places to see buses. Both Ilford and Romford are good for East London, Capital Citybus and Harris Bus operations, while at Barking one can also witness Dennis Darts from Oxford and Docklands Transit, both incidentally, bearing Oxfordshire registrations. Stratford, a little nearer to central London, has a modern open-air bus station, a vast improvement on its subterranean predecessor. Regular operators include Harris Bus, Capital Citybus, East London and Thamesway.

In north London, Golders Green, with its bus station fronting the Northern Line underground station, is always worth a look, with mainly a mixture of Metroline, MTL and CentreWest. The only Routemasters here now are those of London Sovereign on the 13 to Aldwych since the conversion of the 139 to Dennis Dart in March 1998. Another recent change is the loss of the 210 to F. E. Thorpe, a route long associated with Grey-Green's curious short Volvo B10Ms. Golders Green is also a stopping-off point for certain National Express journeys to and from the north.

Lastly, in this brief tour of London, I can recommend Harrow-on-the-Hill, another centre with a number of operators. The main company is Metroline, which has a garage a mile or to the north, at Harrow Weald. However, many local routes are in the hands of Sovereign Harrow, albeit all worked by midibuses. London United put in an appearance on the 140 from Heathrow, often with a route-branded Leyland Olympian, while CentreWest 223 is a midibus route from Wembley. London Sovereign's 114 will usually produce an Olympian, as will Shires' route 340 from Edgware. Another Shires' route, this time using midibuses, is the commercial 350 from Watford Junction. A final splash of colour is provided by the London Buslines' Darts on the 258. Universitybus also work into Harrow, albeit infrequently, on their route 614 from Hatfield and Hertford.

Right: London United Leyland-bodied Leyland Olympian L294 (G294 UYK) is one that carries branding for route 140 (Harrow Weald-Heathrow Airport). It is seen near Harrow town centre in January 1988. *Kevin Lane*

Armchair Passenger Transport Co Ltd
Commerce Way, Brentford, Middlesex, TW8 8LZ

Armchair first began operating London Transport contracts in June 1990, with the award of route 260 (Shepherds Bush-North Finchley). Prior to this, it had been predominantly a coaching firm, although two former Green Line routes had been operated in the late 1980s; and from 1987, some Surrey County Council contracts had been gained.

Since then, other LT contracts have been won: the 65 (Ealing Broadway-Kingston) in January 1991 and more recently, the 117 (Isleworth-Staines) and the 190 (Richmond-West Brompton).

More recent acquisitions are Ealing local routes E2 and E8, both won from CentreWest, and the 237 (Shepherds Bush-Hounslow Heath), won from London United and which began in June 1998. At this date, the 260 passed to Metroline.

In addition, a number of Surrey County Council routes were operated until the summer of 1997.

Current rolling stock comprises mainly Leyland Olympians with Alexander and Leyland bodies, and Plaxton-bodied Dennis Darts. Double-deckers are used on the 65 and 237 (those on the latter formerly on the 260), while Dennis Darts are to be seen on the rest. These are 37-seaters on the 117/190 and 35-seater SLFs on the E2/E8. Several elderly Leyland Atlanteans were replaced by a number of Volvo Olympians with

Northern Counties Palatine II bodywork in 1998. Buses carry an orange and white livery.

Above left: To supplement older Leyland Olympians on route 65 (Kingston-Ealing Broadway Station), four Northern Counties Palatine II-bodied Volvo Olympians were added to the fleet at the end of 1997. No R420 SOY takes on a good load in Kingston in March 1998. **Kevin Lane**

Above: Dennis Darts are scheduled on routes 117, 190, E2 and E8. P154 MLE is a 9.8m SFD412 model, with 37-seat Plaxton Pointer bodywork, one of 13 delivered in 1996. It is seen at Hammersmith Broadway in March 1998 on route 190, heading for West Brompton from Richmond. **Kevin Lane**

Below left: At the time of writing, the 1990 batch of Alexander-bodied Leyland Olympians are on the 260 route, but will switch to the 237 from June 1998. No G366 YUR passes beneath the Hammersmith & City branch of the Metropolitan Line at Shepherds Bush in this March 1998 view. **Kevin Lane**

Below: On crew bus duties at Ealing Broadway is Ford Transit C322 RPE, acquired from London Buslines in 1995, but new to the Berks Bucks Bus Co in 1986. **Kevin Lane**

Arriva Croydon & North Surrey
Lesbourne Road, Reigate, Surrey, RH2 7LE

London & Country was originally known as London Country South West, following the break up of London Country Bus Services in 1986. It was an early operator of LT contracts, taking over route 127 from LCBS, in March 1986. A number of further LT-tendered routes were operated subsequently, including a couple of high-profile routes into central London — the 78 and 176 — both since lost. Under British Bus ownership, its London operations and garages at Croydon, Walworth and Dunton Green were transferred to a new company, Londonlinks Buses Ltd. This took place in January 1995, coming under Kentish Bus management. This left London & Country with few commitments as far as LT work was concerned.

In August 1997, and now part of the Cowie Group, Londonlinks was returned to the London & Country fold, operating as a subsidiary company, but only from Croydon garage. From late 1997 London & Country became part of Arriva plc. The former London Country and Londonlinks operations now come under Arriva Croydon & North Surrey Ltd.

Arriva Croydon & North Surrey operates two trunk routes within the LT network: the 85 (Kingston-Putney Bridge) and 465 (Teddington-Dorking). The former now use the impressive DAFDB250/Northern Counties

Palatine combination which replaced Volvo Citybuses early in 1998, while the 465 is worked by low-floor Dennis Dart SLFs. Both routes operate from Leatherhead garage. Other LT routes are H27, H28, H29, K5, K6, R61, R62 and school route 627. All except the latter run from a base at Hounslow Heath, generally using midibuses, although the H28 (Bull's Bridge-Osterley), uses Dennis Darts. In addition, there are several otherwise commercial routes that are under contract to LT within their area, namely the 406, 408 and 425 into Croydon. London & Country, of course, also works into the LT area on other services to Croydon, Sutton and Kingston on either commercial or Surrey County Council contracts.

The former Londonlinks subsidiary operates from a modern base at Beddington Farm Road, Croydon. Double-deckers with East Lancs bodywork, and Volvo Citybuses with either Northern Counties or East Lancs bodies, the latter coming from the North Western fleet. There are also a couple of former LCBS LR class Leyland Olympians for school work. The double-deck routes are 400 (Wallington-Caterham-on-the-Hill), 403 (West Croydon-Warlingham Park Hospital) and commercial route 409 (West Croydon-East Grinstead).

Below: DSL90 (P290 FPK), a 1997 Dennis Dart SLF/Plaxton Pointer, leaves Surbiton for Teddington on a 465 from Dorking in March 1998. **Kevin Lane**

Top: Adding a splash of green to mainly red-dominated Hounslow is DS18 (N530 SPA), an East Lancs EL2000-bodied Dennis Dart, new in 1995. It is seen in Kingsley Road on the H28 (Osterley, Tesco-Bulls Bridge, Tesco) during a heavy shower of rain, hence the headlights, in March 1998. **Kevin Lane**

Above: In Londonlinks livery at West Croydon is Volvo Olympian/East Lancs 696 (M696 HPF), on a 289 journey from Purley Station to Elmers End. **Kevin Lane**

Of the single-deck routes, the 127 (Tooting Broadway-Purley Station) uses the Volvo B6/Northern Counties, ex-Kentish Bus, while the 289 (Purley Station-Elmers End Green) is in the hands of various Leyland Lynxes, including a couple new to Merthyr Tydfil. The 407 (Sutton-Caterham station) has Dennis Darts as does the 455 (Wallington-Purley), in the latter case red ones, that came with the route from South London. (The 455 was acquired at the same time in July 1997, with South London taking over operation of Londonlinks' 176, then still with Kentish Bus.) Other routes use various Metroriders and Mercedes midibuses, including on commercial routes Croydon area. There is also a commercial route in the Streatham area: the S11 (East Dulwich-Streatham Common).

Below: Also from Londonlinks is Dennis Dart/Northern Counties 121 (L121 YVK), a former Kentish Bus vehicle. The location is Sutton and it is working a 407 from Caterham Station in March 1998. **Kevin Lane**

Right: Thirteen Wright Handybus-bodied Dennis Darts are in stock, including DW314 (J314 XVX) laying over at Turnpike Lane off route 444 from Chingford in April 1998. **Kevin Lane**

Arriva East Herts & Essex Ltd

Harlow Bus Garage, Harlow, Essex, CM20 1YD

ounty Bus & Coach was formed when London ountry North East was divided in 1989, taking the astern half in the Harlow, Hertford and Grays areas. he next year, 1990, saw its entry into LT-tendered ork, to which it still has a small commitment today, lthough a number of other routes enter the London rea from Essex. County became part of the Cowie roup in 1996, subsequently passing to Arriva plc uring the following year. Two events to note during he latter part of 1997 were the acquisition of West's, Voodford, in August and the transfer of the Leaside ravel operations of Leaside Bus Co, also part of rriva. West's ran local services on the north ondon/Essex borders, the final bus fleet including Metroriders, Dennis Darts and two DAF Optare Deltas. he Leaside Travel fleet included Metrobuses, Leyland itans, a couple of Routemasters and a variety of oaches. A green and cream livery is worn, which will e superseded by Arriva turquoise and white in due ourse. The new fleetname is 'Arriva Serving Herts & ssex'.

Seven LT routes are currently operated, the most ecent being the 34 (Barnet church-Walthamstow tation) which was transferred from Leaside in lovember 1997. New Plaxton Pointer-bodied low-floor

Dennis Dart SLFs are scheduled for this service, operating from Edmonton. These replace the Metrobuses formerly turned out by Leaside. Older Plaxton-bodied Darts, together with a couple of Wright-bodied examples, working from Edmonton, appear on routes 444 (Chingford Station-Turnpike Lane Station) and W16 (Chingford Mount-Leytonstone station). Other Plaxton-bodied Darts, dating from 1992/6, work from Grays on routes 256 (Noak Hill-Hornchurch, St Georges Hospital) and 346 (Upminster station-Upminster Park Estate).

The two remaining LT contracts require Mercedes midibuses. Route W14 (Leytonstone-Woodford Bridge) is worked from Debden, an outstation of Harlow, while route W15 (Walthamstow Central Station-Hackney Central Station) is worked from Edmonton. A quartet of Marshall-bodied Ivecos are allocated to Edmonton for LT mobility routes. Numbered MBT713-6 (L713-6 OVX), they sport a red and cream livery.

In addition to the LT routes, Arriva East Herts & Essex works into the London area on a number of other services, commercially operated, but under agreement within the LT area; route 505 for example runs from Harlow to Chingford and Walthamstow.

Above: A W16 from Chingford Mount arrives at Leytonstone station in the care of Dennis Dart DP307 (J307 WHJ) in February 1998. **Kevin Lane.**

Below: Iveco/Marshall mobility bus MBT715 (L715 OVX) keeps an East London Leyland Titan company at Stratford in February 1998. **Kevin Lane**

Above: Leaside Travel vehicles are a familiar sight in London; Bova Futura BOV545 (G545 JOG) proceeds along Buckingham Palace Road in February 1998, possibly to take up service on route 711 to Harlow. *Kevin Lane.*

Below: Sporting the new Arriva Kent Thamesside livery, Volvo Citybus/Northern Counties 7635 (G635 BPH) is one of 13 delivered to London & Country in 1989 but which came from Londonlinks in 1996/97. It works a 272 Woolwich-Thamesmead-Woolwich circular at Woolwich in April 1998. *Kevin Lane*

Arriva Kent Thamesside Ltd
Invicta House, Armstrong Road, Maidstone, Kent, ME15 6TY

When London Country Bus Services was split up in 1986, one of the new companies was given the not particularly imaginative name of London Country South East, which later became Kentish Bus & Coach. Later still, it became part of British Bus, subsequently the Cowie Group and now Arriva plc, where it has become Arriva Kent Thamesside Ltd, trading as 'Arriva Serving Kent Thamesside'. It is managed with Maidstone & District and currently operates from Dartford and Northfleet garages.

Kentish Bus gained itself a high profile in 1990 when it gained routes 22A, 22B and 55 into central London, on which it used new Leyland Olympians in an eye-catching livery of maroon and cream. Its presence in central London was further highlighted in 1992 when it took over route 19, complete with Routemasters hired out from LRT. Numerous other routes were contracted to Kentish Bus in southeast London and the north Kent area. The failure of Boro'line Maidstone in 1992 saw its LT commitments pass to Kentish Bus, while Transcity Link of Sidcup was taken over the following year. In 1995, Kentish Bus took control of a new company — Londonlinks — which had been the London & Country operations from Croydon, Walworth and Dunton Green. However, following dramatic changes within the Cowie (and later Arriva) Group,

Kentish Bus has totally withdrawn from the central London area.

Londonlinks passed back to London & Country in August 1997, followed by the transfer of the 19 and its RMLs to South London in the October. The 227 and 320 passed to Selkent a few weeks later. January 1998 saw the wholesale removal of routes 22A, 22B, 55, 78 and 225, together with their vehicles, to Leaside, while three weeks later the 132 and 233 to Metrobus. Thus, the nearest point to central London now served is Greenwich, on route 286 from Sidcup.

All of this activity has resulted in a fair decrease in vehicles and a retreat back to its more traditional operating area. Operations are now conducted only from Dartford and Northfleet. Of the LT-contracted services, the principal double-deck routes are now the 96 (Woolwich-Dartford) and 272 (Woolwich-Thamesmead-Woolwich). Vehicles are mainly Leyland and Volvo Olympians, together with a few Volvo Citybuses, with bodywork by Northern Counties, East Lancs and Alexander. A handful of former London Country AN-class Leyland Atlanteans also survive at Northfleet.

As far as LT routes are concerned, single-deckers are mainly a mixture of Dennis Darts and Metroriders,

Below: The old Kentish Bus maroon and yellow livery adorns Volvo Olympian/Northern Counties Palatine II 5557 (L557 YCU) arriving in Bromley in April 1998 on a 269 working from Bexleyheath. Kevin Lane

16

Above: Among the buses acquired from Boro'line Maidstone in 1992 were a dozen Optare-bodied Leyland Olympians, new in 1988/89. No 5758 (E158 OMD) was also working the 272 circular in Woolwich in April 1998. **Kevin Lane**

Below: The Dennis Darts on the 286 (Greenwich-Sidcup, Queen Mary's Hospital) are in Arriva colours. No 3179 (P179 LKL) pulls away from Sidcup station in April 1998. **Kevin Lane**

including new SLFs for the 286 (Greenwich-Sidcup), these running in the new Arriva livery. Former Boro'line Leyland Lynxes may be found on route 492 (Sidcup-Dartford), as well as the 428 (Erith-Dartford Station), one of several routes that run into the LT area and are partly contracted by LT. A number of Mobility routes are operated from Northfleet using a trio of wheelchair-fitted Leyland Nationals, originating from Southdown and London Buses.

At the time of writing, spring 1998, buses can be seen running in maroon and yellow, yellow and green and the latest Arriva colours of turquoise and white. Mobility buses are red with white relief.

Left: *A rather damp morning in Bromley High Street in April 1998 sees Northern Counties Paladin-bodied Dennis Dart 3140 (L140 YVK) arriving from Eltham on route 126.*
Kevin Lane

Right: *The livery style prior to that adopted by Arriva was an attractive green and yellow. Optare MetroRider 1852 (N852 YKE) demonstrates this in Orpington on local route R8 in April 1998.*
Kevin Lane

Arriva London North Ltd
16 Watsons Road, Wood Green, London N22 4TZ

Leaside Buses was bought by the Cowie Group on 29 September 1994. Its operating area is northeast London and it has garages at Palmers Green, Tottenham, Clapton, Enfield and Wood Green.

Arriva London North's buses work right into central London, on such routes as the 29 (Wood Green-Trafalgar Square) and the 38 (Clapton Pond-Victoria). The chosen livery was red, with wide diagonal yellow bands at the rear, and a straight yellow band under the windscreen. The Cowie Group restructured itself towards the end of 1997, emerging as Arriva plc, and while regulations will not allow the new Arriva corporate image of turquoise and white to adorn its buses in London, a new revised version has been launched, with the fleetname 'Arriva Serving London'. The new 'circle within a circle' logo is prominently displayed on buses in former liveries.

Although there had been little integration between neighbouring Cowie companies in London, 1997/8 saw a number of interesting developments. October

1997 saw the contraction of the Leaside Travel fleet, a variety of vehicles used for private hire, and other special services which included open-top Leyland Titans, two RMCs and nine coaches, transferred to County Bus at Edmonton. An even greater upheaval was the transfer of the Kentish Bus operations at Cambridge Heath over to Leaside from the beginning of 1998. This involved some 59 buses: five Dennis Darts, 11 Volvo Citybuses, with the remaining vehicles being Leyland Olympians; and routes 22A, 22B, 55, 78 and 225. The depot at Cambridge Heath closed in February 1998.

The Routemaster is currently to be found on routes 38 and 73 (Stoke Newington-Victoria), Mondays to Saturdays. The fleet is mostly RML, including pre-production Nos 882/84/88/96/97, and a few RMs, notably RM5. These are allocated to Tottenham and Clapton garages. The majority of the fleet is made up of the Metrobus, while there are 40 Alexander-bodied Leyland Olympians, numbered L315-54, at Clapton for route 253 (Aldgate-Euston). There is a batch of 13 BS-class Northern Counties-bodied DAF DB250s at Wood Green for route 263 (Archway Station-Barnet General Hospital), new in 1995 when the contract for the route was won from MTL London. More DAFs with Alexander bodies are on order for Metrobus replacement during 1998. The double-deck fleet was swollen with the influx of Kentish Bus vehicles as noted above, although the Volvos subsequently moved on to Grey-Green.

Single-deckers are very much in the minority in the Arriva London North fleet. The most numerous are the LDR class of Dennis Darts, with 40-seat Plaxton Pointer bodywork, new in 1995/6. The 37-strong class is at Wood Green for route 184 (Turnpike Lane Station-Barnet) and Enfield for routes 307 (Brimsdown Station-Barnet) and 313 (Chingford Station-Potters Bar). Other Dennis Darts are four 34-seat Plaxton Pointers at Palmers Green, DRL49-52 for route 298 (Southgate Station-Clare Hall) and DT58-64 bodied by Carlyle at Enfield for route 192 (Enfield Town-Lea Valley Tesco). The aforementioned ex-Kentish Bus Darts were subsequently transferred to Grey Green.

Route 144 (Edmonton Green station-Muswell Hill

Below: Although Routemasters are scheduled only for routes 38 and 73, they can occasionally appear elsewhere. One such occasion was the use of RML2391 (JJD 391D) on route 76 on 27 March 1998, the day before it was transferred, along with the 259, to Capital Citybus. The photographer, unaware of its use on the 76, caught it on the approach to Ludgate Hill, a case of being in the right place at the right time for once!
Kevin Lane

Left: The most numerous type in the Arriva London North, formerly Leaside, fleet are Metrobuses dating from 1978-1986, currently totalling over 300. Among the first to receive the new Arriva livery style for London is M732 (KYV 723X) seen at Edmonton Green in March 1998, working a 149 towards London Bridge Station.
Philip Wallis

Broadway) requires low-floor buses and has them in the shape of Wright-bodied Scania N113s (SLW1-14), delivered shortly before the Cowie takeover. Three additional buses on this route from March 1998 are DAF SB220/Northern Counties DLP1-3 which each have the capacity to carry a wheelchair. Other small buses are a trio of MCW Metroriders (MR102/4/5) used on a contract to shuttle staff around in central London for the Department of Social Security at Waterloo.

Above: Forty Alexander-bodied Leyland Olympians, L315-354, were delivered in 1992 and work on route 253 (Aldgate station-Euston station). L352 (J352 BSH) begins its journey at Aldgate in February 1998. **Kevin Lane**

Right: A small batch of 13 DAF double-deckers with Northern Counties Palatine II bodywork entered the fleet in 1995 for route 263 (Archway station-Barnet General Hospital). DBS8 (N608 DWY) arrives back at Archway in April 1998. **Kevin Lane**

Right: A trio of DAF single-deckers were put into service alongside SLW-class Scanias on route 144 in early 1998. They carry Plaxton Prestige 32-seat dual-door bodywork with chair lift. DLP1 (R151 GNW), devoid of any fleetnames, swings out of Turnpike Lane bus station when still quite new in April 1998. **Kevin Lane**

Arriva London North East Ltd

Stamford Hill Garage, Rookwood Road, London N18 5TD

Grey-Green was a long-established name in bus operation. Formerly part of the George Ewer Group, taken over by the Sunderland-based Cowie Group in 1980, Grey-Green later became part of Arriva plc and was renamed Arriva London North East Ltd, trading as 'Arriva Serving London'. The business was essentially coaching, but in 1987 Grey-Green began running its first LRT-tendered route, the 173, dubbed 'Eastenderbus'. Within a year, a further four routes were being operated in north and east London. However, the winning of route 24 (Hampstead Heath-Pimlico) brought tendering into the heart of London, bringing Grey-Green and a fleet of Volvo Citybuses well and truly into the limelight. Ten years on, 11 daily routes are operated from Stamford Hill and Barking, together with four on schooldays only. From the end of January 1998 changes within Arriva plc included the transfer of ex-Kentish Bus route 78 (Shoreditch High Street-Peckham Rye) from Leaside to Grey-Green, who lost their route 125 (Finchley Central-Winchmore Hill) to Leaside.

Route 24 is still operated using many of the buses that launched the route: dual-door Alexander-bodied Volvo Citybuses. Similar buses can be found on route 168 (Hampstead Heath-Elephant & Castle). Other double-deck Volvos are 11 former coaches, nine Alexander and two East

Lancs, reseated as buses, whose weekday haunt is route 141 (Wood Green station-Moorgate). Scania double-deckers with Northern Counties and East Lancs bodies (including another reseated coach among the latter) total 13, some of which work the 66 (Romford Station-Leytonstone). Fourteen Leyland Olympians with Northern Counties bodywork were added to the fleet when only a few months old, in January 1991. These had come from County Bus & Coach with route 103 (Rainham-North Romford). From Leaside in January 1998 came a batch of 11 Volvo Citybus B10M-50s with Alexander bodies for route 78 (Shoreditch High Street-Peckham Rye). These buses had been new to Boro'line Maidstone and had arrived with Grey-Green via Kentish Bus, Londonlinks, Kentish Bus (again) and Leaside. Not bad for nine-year-old vehicles!

Perhaps the most interesting of the single-deckers are the 13 Volvo B10Ms with East Lancs 41-seat bodies, Nos 912-25. Dating from 1990, they feature a

Right above: Scania N112DRB/East Lancs 113 (F113 KYN) pulls out into traffic in Leytonstone High Road, shortly after leaving the little bus station by the Underground station on route 66 to Romford in January 1998. **Kevin Lane**

Right below: The 141 (Moorgate-Wood Green station) is the preserve of the 1985 Volvo B10Ms rebodied by East Lancs in 1992; No 171 (B871 XYR) in Grey Green livery and with Arriva name and logos, heads north past Turnpike Lane station in April 1998. The short rear overhang is apparent. **Kevin Lane**

Above: No 133 (F133 PHM) is from the first of three batches of Alexander-bodied Volvo Citybuses and dates from 1988. It was seen at Victoria on a Pimlico-bound 24 in January 1998. *Kevin Lane*

long-wheelbase together with a short rear overhang. These were designed to overcome the problem of tight corners encountered on route 210 (Finsbury Park station-Brent Cross), a route on which London Buses had previously used 10.3m Leyland Nationals. This route is due to pass to F. E. Thorpe later in 1998.

Eight Dennis Darts with 31-seat Plaxton Pointer bodies were added to stock in 1993 for route 173 (Goodmayes-East Beckton, Asda), while a ninth, albeit a 40-seater, arrived in 1995. Low-floor Dennis Dart

SLFs, with bodywork by Alexander, came in 1997 for two routes: the 20 (Walthamstow Central station-Debden station) and 167 (Ilford High Road-Debden station), also turning up on the 173 on Sundays. Five Northern Counties Paladin-bodied Darts came from Leaside in February 1998, having come previously from Kentish Bus. Numbered 815-819, they were put to work on route 225 (Lewisham-Rotherhithe), initially in Kentish Bus livery.

Below: Low-floor Dennis Darts work on routes 20 and 167; Alexander-bodied 961 (P961 RUL) picks up passengers at Gants Hill on its way to Ilford in February 1998. *Kevin Lane*

Arriva London South

Croydon Bus Garage, Brighton Road, South Croydon, Surrey CR2 6EL

South London was the final LBL company to be sold, going to the Cowie Group, who had earlier bought Leaside, on 10 January 1995. The Cowie Group adopted a red livery with yellow diagonals towards the rear and a single yellow band under the windscreen. Currently part of Arriva, its 'wheel within wheel' symbol is now displayed. Garages are at Brixton, Croydon, Norwood and Thornton Heath. Long-haul routes into London include the 2 (Crystal Palace-Marylebone) and the 68 (Norwood Garage-Euston). In May 1997 the Cowie Group began to reorganise

various parts of its empire in London, including the transfer of two Londonlinks routes to South London, taking effect from July in the case of the 176 (Penge-Oxford Circus) and August for route 188 (Greenwich-Euston). With these routes came 36 East Lancs-bodied Volvo Citybuses. In the reverse direction, Londonlinks gained South London route 455 (Wallington-Purley Old Lodge Lane), taking with it nine Dennis Darts (DRL201-9). Furthermore, October saw RML route 19 (Battersea Bridge-Finsbury Park) pass to South London from Kentish Bus, the vehicles

Above: Arriva London South is home to over 180 Leyland Olympians. Most have ECW bodywork, illustrated by L259 (D259 FYM) in West Croydon on route 198 (Thornton Heath-Shrublands) in March 1998.
Kevin Lane

Right: Twenty-four former Kentish Bus Olympians are L533-556, transferred from Leaside at the end of February 1998. L546 (G546 VBB) works the 176 towards Penge along the Strand a month later.
Kevin Lane

remaining at Battersea, under Brixton's control.

Much of the current fleet originates from before privatisation, with Routemasters, Leyland Olympians and MCW Metrobuses well to the fore. The transfer of route 19, as mentioned above, has boosted the Routemaster fleet to 81. Both RMs and RMLs are represented: 28 RMs, the remainder RMLs. The RMs are on route 159 (Streatham Station-Baker Street station), while the RMLs can also be found on route 137 (Streatham Hill-Oxford Circus), both Mondays to Saturdays only. Amongst the Routemasters are RM6 and pre-production RMLs (892/95).

A large fleet of over 150 ECW-bodied Leyland Olympians are in service and date from 1984/6/7. There are a number of early examples, including L1-6, the class being allocated to Norwood, Croydon and Thornton Heath. There are also nearly as many Metrobuses, these being at Brixton and Croydon, a few of which are available either as permanent or temporary driver training buses.

The only other double-deckers are the VE class Volvo Citybuses inherited from Londonlinks in 1997, which date from 1990/1, although new buses are currently on order to replace these, in the shape of DAF DB250s with Alexander bodywork.

Single-deckers, as elsewhere in London these days are mainly Dennis Darts. DR20-31 are Plaxton Pointer-bodied examples dating from 1991 and are a Thornton Heath for service on route 249 (Crystal Palace-Tooting Bec Station). The longer DRLs can be found working from all garages except for Brixton, while there are also a few Carlyle-bodied Darts — DTs — at Thornton Heath, where they mix with MRL class MetroRiders on route G1 (Streatham Station-Battersea). Other Darts are 40-seat (LDR22-39), again Plaxton Pointer-bodied, at Brixton for route 319 (Sloane Square-Streatham).

As part of the construction of the Croydon Tramlink the railway line between Wimbledon and West Croydon, operated by Connex South Central, was closed and replaced by buses from June 1997. South London won the tender, and the limited-stop service — numbered TL1 — uses Ikarus-bodied DAF SB220 or Dennis Darts. They were previously with a variety of operators: Grey-Green, County Bus, Birmingham Coach Company and Stuarts, Dukinfield, Greater Manchester.

Below: Formerly with Londonlinks, this Volvo Citybus/East Lancs, VE649 (H649 GPF), is at Elephant & Castle in February 1998 on its way to Euston on a 188 from Greenwich. **Kevin Lane**

Above: This anonymous looking red Dennis Dart is in fact one of London South's, in this case DRL153 (L143 ...G). It is leaving Elephant & Castle on a 322 to Crystal Palace in February 1998. **Kevin Lane**

Below: Eighteen 40-seat Plaxton Pointer-bodied Darts, LDR-class, were new in 1996; LDR30 (P830 RWU) is on ...r regular route, the 319 (Streatham-Sloane Square), at Clapham Junction in April 1998. **Kevin Lane**

Arriva The Shires

Castle Street, Luton, Bedfordshire, LU1 3AJ

Arriva The Shires, formerly Luton and District and now part of the Arriva Group, currently operates three LT-tendered routes. The 142 (Watford Junction-Edgware-Brent Cross) was inherited from London Country North West in 1990, having originated with the old London Country Bus Services in June 1986. The 340 (Edgware station-Harrow) has been operated since January 1991. The most recent tender is that for route U9 (Uxbridge station-Harefield Hospital), won from CentreWest. This was due to commence in June 1998, but was actually begun the previous February, initially using Mercedes hired from CentreWest.

Commercial route 350 runs from Watford Junction to Harrow, under an agreement with LT, while routes B1/2, B4/5/6 and B9 run on the LT borders at Borehamwood. Other local routes run into the LT area at Northwood and Uxbridge, while a comprehensive local and limited-stop network is operated through Bedfordshire, Buckinghamshire and Hertfordshire.

As far as the 142, 340 and 350 are concerned, the latter is midibus operated, in this case Mercedes-Benz Varios with Plaxton Beaver bodies. The two tendered routes require Leyland Olympians, supplied by Garston garage.

The current livery is blue and yellow, to be superseded by the new Arriva corporate image of turquoise and cream. The new fleetname is 'Arriva Serving The Shires'.

Left: Leyland Olympian/Alexander 5130 (F747 XCS), leaves Edgware for Brent Cross on route 142 from Watford Junction in October 1997. The 142 was originally contracted London Country Bus Services in June 1986, subsequently passing to London Country North West and Luton & District. No 5130 was new to A1 Service, Ardrossan in 1989 and acquired by Luton & District in 1995. **Kevin Lane**

Left: Also at Edgware in October 1997, this time at the bus station, is Leyland-bodied Leyland Olympian 5126 (H1.. GRO), new in 1991, taking on passengers towards Harrow, on route 340. **Kevin Lane**

Capital Citybus Ltd

ry Road, Dagenham, Essex, RM9 6QD

yellow buses of Capital Citybus are a familiar
nt in many areas of north and east London and
bining parts of Essex, operating both tendered and
mercial services. The company was preceded by
ign Bus, who had won its first LRT tender back in
6 and soon grew to be a major operation in east
don/Essex. At the end of 1990 EnsignBus was sold
long Kong Citybus, resulting in a change of name
livery, the former blue and silver being replaced
yellow. In 1991, London Forest, one of the London
units, was unable to take up contracts due to
ustrial problems to the benefit of Capital Citybus,
ulting in a virtual doubling of the business. After
years, at the end of 1995, the company was sold
k to its management.

e fleet has always been an interesting one, with a
mix of new and second-hand rolling stock. These
ently operate from three bases: Dagenham Dock,
thumberland Park and Hackney Wick. While some
es are allocated to specific routes, in many cases a
ety of double-deckers may be used.

th the exception of a pair of Routemasters
120/1913) generally used on special duties, the
est of the double-deckers are Metrobuses dating
n 1980/1 and originating from London General,
ester, Badgerline, South Yorkshire and a single

example from Derby. The three from Badgerline,
acquired from Merseyside, have dual-purpose seating.
Four formerly operated in London by Metroline at
Harrow and the last Metrobus 2 to be built for West
Midlands Travel, but not delivered, are also in stock. A
batch bought new in 1988 are numbered 297-91/3/4.

Olympians, of both Leyland and Volvo varieties, are
in the fleet in some numbers, with bodywork by
Alexander, Northern Counties and one by Optare. Most
are bought new, but several have come south from
Highland Scottish and one (250) was a former
demonstrator. As the Olympians used on the 91
(Crouch End Broadway-Trafalgar Square) work in to
central London, they carry a mainly red livery,
although with yellow relief. This is the newest batch
(223-38), delivered early in 1997 and bodied by
Alexander (Belfast). One of these, 238, carries an
experimental rear destination display, identical to, and
as comprehensive as, that at the front.

The Dennis Dominator is also a numerous type in the
Capital Citybus fleet. Bodywork variety is supplied by
Alexander, Northern Counties and East Lancs, while
second-hand members of the fleet have come from
Leicester, Southampton, Kelvin Central (new to
Merseyside) and Mainline. Of particular note are the
pair acquired from London Coaches in 1993, having

*ow: Dennis Arrows have been entering the fleet since 1996. Nos 401-16 have Northern Counties Palatine II
ywork, as fitted to 408 (P408 PLE) arriving in Barking on a 179 journey from Chingford in February 1998.
in Lane*

started life with London Buses in 1984 as H2-3, one of the classes involved in the Alternative Vehicle Evaluation Trials during 1985. Furthermore, 24 Northern Counties-bodied Dominators were bought new in 1991.

The latest double-deckers are Dennis Arrows with Northern Counties single-door (401-416), and East Lancs dual-door bodywork (417-26). Later vehicles, numbered from 427-53, are in red livery for routes 76 (Lea Valley Tesco-County Hall) and 259 (Enfield-Holborn Circus), taken over from Leaside in March 1998.

Single-deckers are in the minority in the fleet, but are an interesting selection nevertheless. Oldest are a small collection of Leyland National 2s, acquired from British Airways, Bluebird and one, 744, former LS454, from Leaside Buses. For schoolbus duties, a pair of

1986 Volvo B10M/Duple buses came from Eastbourn 10 years later, while new vehicles include Mercedes 811Ds, Optare MetroRiders and Volvo B6s, the latter on route 236 (Finsbury Park Station-Hackney Wick) and D5 (Mile End Station-Crossharbour).

Despite their popularity elsewhere in London, only a few Dennis Darts are currently in stock. Nos 669-70 are bodied by Wadham Stringer and Northern Counties respectively. The former came from Wealde in Kent, the latter was bought new. Nos 705-17 are Dart SLFs with East Lancs Spryte bodywork, to be seen on route S2 (Stratford-Clapton). Also noteworth are 701-4, Optare Excel 33-seaters, used on route 396 (Ilford Broadway-Goodmayes). Lastly, there are eight non-PSV status Ford Transit minibuses, acquire from a variety of sources, and used as staff buses.

Above: *Subsequent deliveries of Dennis Arrows have East Lancs bodies of a more angular style. No 422 (P422 PVW) is in Ilford on a 36. to Thames View Estate in February 1998.* **Kevin Lane**

Left: *Alexander (Belfast)-bodied Volvo Olympian 238 (P238 MPU) is one of the vehicles that carries a largely red livery for use on central London route 91 (Crouch End Broadway-Trafalgar Square). It is seen in the Caledonian Road on a sunny February morning in 1998.* **Kevin Lane**

Above: Twenty-four Northern Counties-bodied Dennis Dominators of 1990/91 are numbered 251-274. No 265 (H265 KVX) pulls out of the bus station at Walthamstow working from Chingford to Leyton in November 1996. **Kevin Lane**

Right: Also on the 91, on a rather cloudier day in March 1998 is 319 (KYV 769X), one of a number of former London General MCW Metrobuses acquired during the previous month. It is seen at Trafalgar Square with an older Metrobus, still with London General, following. **Kevin Lane**

Right below: Among the older vehicles in the Capital Citybus fleet are a number of Leyland National 2s, four of which came from British Airways, Heathrow in 1993. No 750 (NLP 389V) is seen leaving Barking on commercial route 348 to Lakeside in March 1998. **Kevin Lane**

Capital Logistics

Sipson Road, West Drayton, Middlesex

Capital Logistics has a very large fleet of buses and coaches, used on various duties such as car-park and hotel transfers at Gatwick and Heathrow Airports. Choice examples include Hispano-bodied DAFs from Singapore, Scanias with Van-Hool dual-purpose bodies and a selection of Leyland Nationals. Formerly Capital Coaches, the name was changed to Capital Logistics in October 1997 following the takeover of Whytes Airport Services, who ran a fleet mainly consisting of DAF Optare Deltas and Fords.

The first tendered route, the H26 (Feltham to Hatton Cross via Heathrow), a Monday to Saturday service, was taken up in August 1993. Three vehicles are required for the service, drawn from five Plaxton Beaver-bodied Mercedes-Benz 709/711Ds, seating variously 18 or 20 and fitted with chair-lifts. The vehicles are in a basic white livery. The H24, which only runs on Sunday afternoons in Feltham, began in March 1998.

A third contract was taken up in April 1998, that of route 726 (Heathrow-Dartford). This limited-stop service had been operated by London Coaches since 1992 using Ikarus-bodied DAF SB220s, the same vehicles being used initially by Capital Logistics. A further LT contract commenced in May 1998, for the U3 (Heathrow Airport-Uxbridge), using Optare Excels, while a further route has been gained, to start in the summer of 1998. This is route 60 (Streatham-Old Coulsdon), formerly operated by South London and will require low floor double-deckers.

*Left: Mercedes 18-seat midibuses are used on their H26 route; P255 MLE is a Plaxton Beaver-bodied 711D, seen on layover at Hatton Cross in March 1998. **Kevin Lane***

*Left: 4 April 1998 saw the takeover by Capital Logistics of limited stop route 726 from London Coaches (Kent). On the first day of the service, Ikarus-bodied DAF SB220 No 4 (J804 KHD) pulls out into traffic in Bromley, heading for Heathrow Airport. **Kevin Lane***

CentreWest London Buses Ltd

Telstar House, Eastbourne Terrace, Paddington, London W2 6LG

CentreWest was sold to its management on 1 September 1994, passing to FirstBus in March 1997. Its operating area is west London, with garages at Acton, Alperton, Greenford, Uxbridge and Westbourne Park. However, there is also a garage at St Mary Cray in Kent, the result of successful tendering in the Orpington area, when five routes were gained in 1995, at the expense of Metrobus and Stagecoach Selkent. Each garage has its own local identity, displayed on its vehicles: 'Ealing Buses' (Acton and Greenford), 'Challenger' (Alperton) and 'Gold Arrow' (Westbourne Park), while those at Uxbridge and Orpington are simply 'Uxbridge Buses' and 'Orpington Buses' respectively. FirstBus, following its involvement with rail transport, is now known as FirstGroup and its symbol, incorporating the letter 'f', is being applied to vehicles after the fleetname.

Routemasters are required for two routes: 7 (Russell Square-East Acton) and 23 (Liverpool Street station-Westbourne Park station), Mondays to Saturdays, but not evenings. These are all RMLs (including RML885, one of the pre-production batch) and are allocated to Westbourne Park garage. In addition, there is open-top RMC1510 and de-licensed RM1492/1676 and RMC1492.

The most common double-decker is the MCW Metrobus, of which over 100 are currently in stock and are scheduled for service at all garages except Greenford and Orpington. All other double-deckers are Olympians of various types. LA and LN classes, Leyland Olympians with either Alexander or Northern Counties bodywork, are at Alperton for route 83 (Golders Green-Ealing Hospital). These buses came from London Buslines, swapped for Dennis Dart SLFs, the transaction being completed in September 1997. Volvo Olympians with Northern Counties bodywork are V1-12/41-55, dating from 1995/6. The first batch is allocated to Orpington for route 61 (Bromley North Station-Chislehurst), while the others are at Uxbridge for limited-stop route 607 (Shepherds Bush Green-Uxbridge), and are branded as such. They are also seen on night route N207.

There is more variety among the single-deck types, although the ubiquitous Dennis Dart is much in evidence. The oldest by far is RF326, preserved by the company and dating from 1952. Other elderly saloons are a number of Bristol LH/ECW and Leyland National 2s in use as driver training vehicles, while one of the Bristols, BL85, is licensed for service at Westbourne Park and carries a cream and brown livery. Uxbridge

Below: The 607 Express (Shepherds Bush Green-Uxbridge station) is the preserve of a batch of Volvo Olympians with Northern Counties Palatine II bodies, V41-55, new in 1996. V44 (P244 UCW) turns at the Green before returning to Uxbridge in March 1998. **Kevin Lane**

has three Leyland Lynxes allocated for route 222 (Hounslow-Uxbridge Station), most workings of which are in the hands of LLWs as noted below, and Buckinghamshire County Council route 335.

The last buses to be delivered to CentreWest before privatisation were a batch of 14 low-floor Dennis Lance SLFs with Wright Pathfinder B34D bodywork, LLW11-24. The rest of these vehicles went to London United (LLW1-10) and Metroline (LLW25-38). LLW11-24 are allocated to Uxbridge for route 222.

The oldest of the midibuses are the MA class of Mercedes-Benz 811D with Alexander bodywork, dating from 1988-9, to be found working at Uxbridge, Greenford and Alperton. MA3-7 at Greenford are fitted with wheelchair lifts for Ealing route E3. However, many of these are due for replacement during the spring of 1998, when there will be a cascading of

Dennis Darts following the arrival of new SLFs. Other older midibuses are the RW class, Wright-bodied Renault S75s, new in 1990. These are scheduled for service only at Greenford, for routes 195 and 282. Of a similar vintage to the MA and RW classes is lone MT8, a wheelchair-accessible Reeve Burgess Beaver-bodied Mercedes-Benz 709D. Another single-member class is MW17, a Wright-bodied Mercedes-Benz 811 acquired from London General in 1993.

There are several further classes of small vehicles to note before we reach the Darts. Ten members of the MM class, Marshall-bodied Mercedes-Benz 811Ds, work in the Orpington area on routes R3/4 and 336, with a further pair, this time of the Vario 0.814D variety, at Uxbridge, on Hertfordshire County Council route R1 (Uxbridge-Mount Vernon Hospital). Ten-seater LDV 400/Crystal minibuses, with wheelchair access

Right: The other members of the V class are at Orpington, where they work on the 61 (Chislehurst-Bromley North). V4 (N304 JBV) splashes along Bromley High Street in April 1998. This vehicle had been de-roofed during an accident at Orpington station and was out of service between September 1997 and January 1998. Kevin Lane

e LC1-3, allocated to Westbourne Park. Marshall
minibuses of the ML class are currently in the course
delivery.

ennis Darts total over 200 with the latest deliveries
counting for around half the fleet. Delivered
tween 1990 and 1993, the Wright-bodied DW class
the oldest and most numerous class. They are
ostly to be found working routes from Westbourne
rk garage, although a few work from Alperton on
utes 224/226 and Park Royal local route PR1. In
dition, they are due to replace MAs in the spring of
98 which will find them also at Greenford and
bridge. An interesting operation is the use of the
ass on night route N31 (Camden Town circular via
nsington), all other night routes in London being
uble-deck.

he year 1995 saw the arrival of the 32-strong DP
ass, Plaxton Pointer-bodied Darts, seating 32 and

distributed between Orpington and Alperton garages.
A smaller class of Darts was delivered in 1996 — the
37-seat Plaxton Pointer-bodied D class — numbering
just nine vehicles, and these are used at Uxbridge on
the 331 (Uxbridge Station-Ruislip station) and
Orpington local route R9. Further low-floor buses —
Plaxton Pointer-bodied Dennis Dart SLFs (L1-6) —
were added to the fleet in 1997 at Uxbridge. These
are dedicated to route A10 (Uxbridge station-
Heathrow Airport). They wear a blue and yellow livery.
Also in 1997 came the Marshall-bodied DM class of
Dart SLFs, numbered DM117-57. All are at Greenford
for Ealing local routes E3, E7, E9 (and E1 on Sundays),
replacing members of the MA and RW classes. Also of
note is DLP1 at Westbourne Park, another Dennis Dart
SLF, but with Plaxton Pointer B27D bodywork. This
vehicle is on long-term loan from London Transport.

*Below: G53 XLO, fleetnumber LA53, is an Alexander RL-bodied Leyland
Olympian, one of those transferred from London Buslines in 1997. It is seen
waiting to pull out into traffic at Ealing Broadway in March 1998.* **Kevin Lane**

*ft: RML2522 (JJD 522D),
aring its FirstGroup identity,
ads west at Ludgate Hill on
23 from Liverpool Street to
dbrook Grove in March
98.* **Kevin Lane**

*ght: Some 112 Metrobuses
ere in stock early in 1998,
cluding M898 (A898 SUL) on
over at Euston Station
ving arrived on an 18 from
dbury in April of that year.
evin Lane*

LONDON LIVERIES

ARMCHAIR

Above: A pair of Armchair Leyland-bodied Leyland Olympians, H557 GKX leading, stand on layover at Ealing Broadway while working on route 65 to Kingston in March 1998.
Kevin Lane

Top Right: Arriva Croydon & North Surrey consists of the former London & Country and Londonlinks operation. LSL9 (N527 SPA) is a Wright Pathfinder-bodied Dennis Lance SLF, one of five delivered in 1994/95. They are used on route 408 from West Croydon to Guildford, contracted to LT within their area. LSL9 catches the spring sunshine as it leaves West Croydon in March 1998.
Kevin Lane

Bottom Right: From the Londonlinks fleet is Optare MetroRider 442 (M442 HPF), passing through East Croydon on its way from Bromley North to West Croydon on route 367 also in March 1998.
Kevin Lane

Left: Low floor Wright-bodied Dennis Lances work route 222 from Uxbridge to Hounslow. LLW19 (ODZ 8919) pauses to set down at Hounslow West station in March 1998. *Kevin Lane*

Below left: Route 282 (Mount Vernon Hospital-Ealing Hospital) gained Marshall-bodied Dennis Dart SLFs from December 1997. DML176 (R176 TLM) heads towards Ealing at Northwood at the beginning of January 1998, still to receive fleetnames. *Kevin Lane*

Below: The six members of the L-class of Plaxton Pointer-bodied Dennis Darts are finished in a blue and yellow livery for route A10, an express facility between Uxbridge and Heathrow Airport. L6 (P406 MLA) sits at Heathrow in March 1998. *Kevin Lane*

Crystals Coaches

27 Dartford Road, Crayford, Kent

Although Crystals had been a minibus operator since 1972, it was only in August 1986 that it really came to the attention of the enthusiast, when it won the LRT contract to operate route 146 (Bromley North-Downe). A Leyland Cub was initially used, followed by a couple of Optare StarRiders when the contract was retained in 1988. However, the route was lost to Metrobus three years later.

Crystals made a re-entry into LT-tendered work with the acquisition of routes R2 (Petts Wood station-Biggin Hill Valley) and R7 (Petts Wood Station-St Mary Cray). A variety of Crystal-bodied Mercedes midibuses are used on these two routes and there are several fitted with chair-lifts for use on the network of Mobility routes operated from bases at Dartford and Chelsea. Buses on LT routes R2 and R7 are an attractive turquoise, while those on mobility work are red and yellow.

Left: Orpington is served by Crystal routes R2 and R7; Mercedes-Benz 709D N602 JGP is working an R7 (Petts Wood Station-St Mary Cray) in the High Street in April 1998. **Kevin Lane**

Below: Crystals also work a number of mobility routes for London Transport. Mercedes-Benz 711D P348 HKU heads towards Orpington on route 971 in Bromley in April 1998. **Kevin Lane**

ARRIVA EAST HERTS & ESSEX

ARRIVA KENT THAMESSIDE

Top Left: *Arriva East Herts & Essex, formerly County Bus & Coach, works the W14 (Leytonstone-Woodford Bridge) from its base at Debden. This is an outstation of Harlow, hence the 'Townlink' fleetname. MB934 (J934 WHJ), a 1991 Plaxton Beaver-bodied Mercedes-Benz 709D loads at Leytonstone Bus Station on a bleak morning in February 998.* **Kevin Lane**

Bottom Left: *The new Arriva image is displayed on Optare MetroRider M445 HPF, 1445 in the Arriva Kent Thamesside fleet. It is sitting off service outside Orpington station in the company of Metrobus Optare Excel 504 (P504 DUG) leaving for Crystal Palace and a London Central Volvo Olympian NV25 (N425 JBV), arriving from Woolwich on route 51.* **Kevin Lane**

Above: *An earlier Kentish Bus livery is carried by Optare-bodied Leyland Olympian 5760 (E160 OMD), originally a Boro'line Maidstone vehicle. The location is Thomas Street, Woolwich and the bus is at the beginning of its journey on route 422 to Bexleyheath in April 1998.* **Kevin Lane**

East London Bus & Coach Co Ltd (Stagecoach East London)

2-4 Clements Road, Ilford, Essex IG1 1BA

Above: East London RML2456 (JJD 456D) was a Country Area bus when new over 30 years ago. It swings out of Paddington on an eastbound 15 in April 1998. **Kevin Lane**

Stagecoach Holdings bought East London, together with Selkent, on 6 September 1994. With 590 vehicles, East London was second only to London General in fleet size. Stagecoach inherited a varied fleet, heavily dominated by the Leyland Titan, a type associated with this part of London since its introduction in 1978. Sixty-one Routemasters were also in the fleet, mainly RMLs but also a handful of RM/RMA/RMC variants. The only other double-deck types then in the fleet were two batches of Scania N113DRBs and a single Optare Spectra — SP2. Single-deckers included Optare Deltas and StarRiders, Dennis Darts and MCW Metroriders, while a trio of coaches consisted of a pair of Leyland Tigers and a Volvo B10M. Furthermore, a batch of low-floor Scanias was in the course of delivery, although only one, SLW15, was actually in stock at the time of takeover.

East London's operating area stretches from central London out to Essex, being prominent in such areas as Ilford, Barking, Romford and Docklands. Garages are at Barking, Bow, Leyton, Romford, Stratford and Upton Park. Long-haul routes include the 15 (Paddington-East Ham), 25 (Oxford Circus-Ilford High Road) and night route N8 (Trafalgar Square-Woodford). Its position in Docklands was consolidated in July 1997 with the acquisition by Stagecoach Holdings of Docklands

Transit, who had been operating as Docklands Minibus. In all, 48 vehicles and four LT-tendered routes were transferred to East London control. The base at Silvertown was closed in the October.

Routemasters are still available for service at Bow and Upton Park garages, Monday to Saturday, on routes 8 (Victoria Station-Bow Church) and 15 (Paddington-Canning Town). RMLs are in the majority and include pre-production RML886/90/98, although there are also five RMs, and three RMCs. One of the latter, RMC1461, has been finished in 1960s' Green Line coach livery and can be seen (and sampled!) on route 15. The other Routemasters carry relief and Stagecoach fleetnames in gold; a nice touch.

The Leyland Titan is still very prominent in the fleet, although withdrawals are taking place, often to other parts of the Stagecoach empire. Notable are a number of the original Titans still in service, including five of the first six to enter service in December 1978, all now at Romford. Several are in use as driver trainers, while T512 is now open-top. T63/80 have dual purpose seating as does T1128, its 630 DYE registration concealing its origins with West Midlands PTE, one of five bought by London Transport back in 1984.

The 50 Scania N113DRBs taken over at privatisation are at Upton Park and Leyton, working a number of

outes from these garages. Nos S22-29 have
Alexander RH bodywork, the remainder with Northern
Counties Palatine bodies, and were new in 1991/2. All
new double-deckers bought under Stagecoach have
been Volvo Olympians. In 1996 the first of the Northern
Counties-bodied VN class arrived for route 374 (Harold
Hill-Romford station). Since then, more have entered
the fleet, working from Romford, Upton Park, Bow and
Romford. The other class of Volvo Olympians, the VA,
has Alexander bodywork, the first arriving during the
summer of 1997.

There is a fair amount of variety within the single-
deck fleet, although much of this is within the ranks of
the Dennis Dart. The DAF Optare Delta is not too
common in London, although East London has the
most, with 26 in stock. DA10 was a demonstrator for
Optare, being two years old when it came to London in
1991. DA11-29 were delivered in 1992, DA30-35 in
1993. They are used on routes 145/169 from Barking.

The year 1993 also saw the arrival at East London of
the first three classes of Dennis Darts. The DRLs, with
Plaxton Pointer 34-seat bodies, work from Barking,
Upton Park and Stratford. DRL121 is in blue livery for a
Tesco supermarket contract, while DRL125/6 wear
London City Airport livery, also blue, as spare vehicles
to the LCY class on this service. Wright-bodied Darts
form the DW (29-seat) and DWL (35-seat) classes, all
at Stratford.

Another pre-privatisation class is the SR —
Mercedes-Benz 811D Optare StarRiders — new in
1988/9. Many wore an orange livery for East London
rail-replacement services ELS/ELT, but this service was
withdrawn in March 1998. The remaining seven are
available for the P14, the only route to run through the
Rotherhithe Tunnel, and includes SR1, carrying its third
registration, E155 CGJ. There are also a handful of
Metroriders, three of which are crewbuses at Stratford.
The only other bus still in the fleet dating from before
the Stagecoach takeover is SLW15, the first Wright
Pathfinder-bodied low-floor
Scania N113. It was joined
by SLW16-30 during
September and October

1994. They are all at Upton Park for route 101 (North
Woolwich-Wanstead station), a service on which they
replaced Leyland Titans.

Further Dennis Darts have been bought by
Stagecoach for East London since 1994. DAL1-27, the
Alexander-bodied DAL class, were new towards the
end of 1995 and are at Barking and Romford for
routes 62 and 247 respectively. Low-floor Darts with
Alexander bodies form two classes: SLDs are at Leyton
and Barking for routes 230 and 264, and a batch of
seven dedicated for the service from Liverpool Street
to London City Airport via Canary Wharf, formerly
operated by D. & J. International, are in a dark blue
livery. These vehicles are classified LCY, perhaps
harking back to the designation of the ex-British
Airways Routemasters as RMA.

Dennis Darts with Plaxton Pointer-bodywork, dual-
doored PDs, were put to work in October 1997 on the
106 (Finsbury Park Station-Whitechapel Station), a
route formerly operated by Docklands Transit. This was
previously in the hands of its own Darts, subsequently
transferred away to Barking, where they may turn up
on the other three former Docklands Transit routes.
These Darts, also Plaxton Pointer, but with single
doors, are the only vehicles from the Docklands Transit
fleet to remain with East London. The Ford Transits
went to a dealer, while the Mercedes-Benz 811Ds
stayed within Stagecoach but in Scotland. The PD
class was expanded at the beginning of 1998 with the
arrival of a batch from Stagecoach Oxford, the former
Thames Transit operation. Alexander-bodied SLFs,
numbered SLD30-50, are the latest Darts; they were
introduced onto the 100 and 276 during the spring of
1998.

To round off the fleet, mention must be made of the
three coaches, available for private hire etc: VP4/5/7
are three Plaxton-bodied Volvo B10M-60s, new to
Wallace Arnold Coaches in 1991. They are allocated to
Romford.

*Right: The fleet of Leyland
Titans is still large; on
layover at Walthamstow
are T473 (KYV 473X) and
T636 (NUW 636Y), both
between duties on route
58 to East Ham.*
Kevin Lane

ARRIVA LONDON N.E.

ARRIVA LONDON NORTH

Top Left No 732 (F112 TML), one of Arriva London North-East's much travelled Volvo Citybuses, picks up passengers at Minories on former Kentish Bus route 78 (Peckham Rye-Shoreditch High Street) in February 1998. The bus wears the livery of a previous owner, namely Londonlinks. **Kevin Lane**

Bottom Left Two Arriva London North Alexander-bodied Leyland Olympians, L333 and L352 (J433/352 BSH), sit at the bus station at Aldgate laying over on route 253 journeys. They both wear the old Cowie Leaside livery style, but with Arriva logos. Keeping them company in this February 1998 view is Capital Citybus 245 (P245 HMD), also a Volvo Olympian, but with Northern Counties bodywork, laying over on route 67. **Kevin Lane**

Below: Showing no sign of its new identity, Arriva London South, ECW-bodied Leyland Olympian L113 (C113 CHM) is seen in the Strand in March 1998, working towards Oxford Circus on route 176 from Penge. **Kevin Lane**

ARRIVA LONDON SOUTH

Left: Alexander RL-bodied Volvo Olympians are now entering the fleet in some numbers. VA58 (R158 VPU) was in Ilford in this February 1998 view. **Kevin Lane**

Right: The DAF Optare Delta is not too common in London, but East London have the most, at 26, numbered DA10-35. DA20 (J720 CYG) waits at Leytonstone for custom on the 145 to Dagenham on a cold February morning in 1998. **Kevin Lane**

Left: London City Airport dedicated Alexander-bodied Dennis Dart SLF, LCY2 (P802 NJN) passing through Limehouse in March 1998. **Kevin Lane**

Right: The ranks of Dennis Darts have been swelled by vehicles from Docklands Transit and Stagecoach Oxford. PD713 (L713 JUD) is from the latter source, and had been newly acquired when seen in Barking in late-February 1998. **Kevin Lane**

Epsom Buses
Blenheim Road, Epsom, Surrey, KT19 9AF

The long-established firm of H. R. Richmond, trading as Epsom Coaches, began bus operation from deregulation in 1986, operating local routes in the Epsom and Croydon area. LT contract work was begun in October 1997 with the takeover of route S1 (Beddington Corner-Banstead), from London General due to staff shortages. A month later Epsom Buses took over another London General route, the 413 (Morden-Sutton), in both cases using Metroriders from London General (MRL179-189). A new route — S4 (Sutton-Roundshaw) — also began in November 1997, with three new 27-seat Mercedes/UVG Citistars.

A new route for 1998 was the 463 (Coulsdon-Wallington), which began at the end of January and replaced much of London & Country's former route 301. Two Dennis Darts are required, drawn from the main fleet. Vehicles are cream with a maroon skirt.

Above: Optare Metrorider H687 YGO, at Sutton station working route S1 (Banstead-Beddington Corner) in March 1998. Both the route and vehicle came from London General. **Kevin Lane**

Right: Mercedes-Benz 709D with Marshall bodywork K593 BEG arriving in Kingston from Epsom on route K9 in March 1998. **Kevin Lane**

45

CAPITAL CITYBUS

CAPITAL LOGISTICS

Above: Laying over at Ealing Broadway in March 1998 is CentreWest DM134 (P134 NLW), one of a growing number of Marshall-bodied Dennis Dart SLFs in the fleet.
Kevin Lane

Top Left Cranbrook Road, Ilford is the setting for Capital Citybus Optare Excel 701 (P701 HMT), running in from Goodmayes on route 396 in February 1998.
Kevin Lane

Bottom Left Capital Logistics took over the limited stop 726 (Heathrow Airport-Dartford) from London Coaches on 4 April 1998 using the same vehicles. On the first day and looking unchanged from the day before, Ikarus-bodied DAF J805 KHD pauses in the rain at Bromley Market, Dartford-bound.
Kevin Lane

Harris Bus Co Ltd

Parker House, Manor Road, West Thurrock, Essex, RM16 1EH

Harris Bus, having previously operated a number of routes in Essex from its West Thurrock base, gained their first LT contracts during 1997. The first was the 108 (Lewisham-Stratford), previously operated by Kentish Bus, who had taken it over from Boro'line Maidstone when they had ceased trading in 1992. For this, Harris is using Optare Excel single-deckers.

In July 1997 Harris Bus took over from Stagecoach East London on three LT routes: 128 (Ilford-Romford), 129 (Claybury Broadway-Becontree Heath) and 150 (Ilford-Chigwell Row). These are all double-deck routes, on which Harris is using East Lancs Pyoneer-bodied Volvo Olympians, together with a pair of DAF SB250/Northern Counties.

Early in 1998 two further routes were added: the 132 (Eltham-Bexleyheath) and 180 (Lewisham-Thamesmead East), previously operated by Kentish Bus and Stagecoach Selkent respectively. The 132 uses more Optare Excels, while the 180 is double-decked, also using further East Lancs Pyoneer-bodied Volvo Olympians. This expansion into north Kent has seen the opening of a new depot in Belvedere.

Apart from services in Essex, Harris also operates a couple of routes from north Kent to the Lakeside shopping centre as well as other services, such as car park shuttles at peak shopping periods. Livery is blue and green and displays various local identities, such as 'Ilford Link' and 'Lewisham Link'.

Below: No 371 (R371 DJN) is one of 35 Volvo Olympians with East Lancs Pyoneer bodywork delivered in 1997/1998. It is seen in Woolwich working route 180 towards Thamesmead East in April 1998, a couple of months after taking over the contract for the service from Stagecoach Selkent. **Kevin Lane**

Above right: No 337 (P337 ROO), is one of half a dozen Northern Counties Palatine II-bodied DAFs in the Harris Bus fleet. It is working on route 129 in Gants Hill in February 1998. **Kevin Lane**

Below: Optare Excels are in favour for single-deck duties; No 334 (P334 NHJ) swings out of Stratford Bus Station heading for Lewisham via the Blackwall Tunnel on route 108 in February 1998. **Kevin Lane**

CENTRE WEST

Above: CentreWest DP15 (N815 FLW), one of a class of 32 Plaxton Pointer-bodied 9-metre Dennis Darts delivered in 1995, at work in Orpington on local route R9 in April 1998. *Kevin Lane*

Below: East London still have a sizeable Leyland Titan fleet. Leyland-bodied T588 (NUW 588Y) turns into London Bridge Station, terminus of the 48 from Walthamstow Central in February 1998. *Kevin Lane*

EAST LONDON

HARRIS BUS

Above: Another operator of the Optare Excel in east London is Harris Bus, with 23 currently in stock. No 330 (P330 NHJ) is at Stratford Bus Station having worked through the Blackwall Tunnel from Lewisham on route 108 in February 1998. **Kevin Lane**

Below: Limebourne Travel gained the C3 (Earls Court-Clapham Junction) from London General in November 1997. Initially they are using Marshall Minibuses on loan from London General until more low-floor Dennis Darts are delivered. ML5 (P505 HEG) is at Earls Court station in March 1998. **Kevin Lane**

LIMEBOURNE TRAVEL

Limebourne Travel

Silverthorne Road, Battersea, London SW8 3HE

Part of Q-Drive and more associated with its coaching activities, Limebourne also operates four LT routes under contract to London Transport. Its first route was the C10 (Victoria Station-Elephant & Castle), gained from London General in 1996 and using Optare MetroRiders. This was followed during 1997 by the 42 (Liverpool Street-Denmark Hill), gained from Kentish Bus and the 156 (Wimbledon-Clapham Junction), also previously operated by London General. Both services are run with low-floor Dennis Darts. The latest route to

be gained by Limebourne is former London General C1 (Earls Court-Clapham Junction), which got underway i November 1997 after London General gave it up due to staff shortages. Six Marshall 29-seaters are being loaned by London General (ML1-6) for around six months to work the service, pending the delivery of more low-floor Darts.

Appropriate to its central London operations, a basic red livery is carried, with a white fleetname over a green block. Vehicles work from the base in Battersea.

Left: Dennis Dart SLF/Plaxton Pointe. P306 HDP, leaves Liverpool Street station at the start of its journey south of the river on route 42 to Denmark Hill in February 1998. The 42 was previously operated by Kentish Bus. **Kevin Lane**

Left: Optare MetroRiders, bought new in 1996, are used on the C10 between Elephant & Castle and Victoria. N206 MWW is seen at the Elephant, also in February 1998. **Kevin Lane**

London Buslines

Middlesex Business Centre, Bridge Road, Southall, Middlesex UB2 4AB

London Buslines, the operating name of Len Wright Travel, Isleworth, was in at the very beginning of LT tendering in July 1985 when he put his yellow DMSs onto the 81 (Hounslow-Slough). Although this route was lost to Westlink in 1995, five LT tenders are currently worked, together with over a dozen mobility routes and some evening and Sunday-only tenders for Surrey County Council. London Buslines are part of FirstGroup under CentreWest Ltd.

With three exceptions, the current fleet consists entirely of Dennis Darts, following the dispersal of double-deckers — all Leyland Olympians — in 1997, mainly going to CentreWest. Plaxton Pointer-bodied

Darts, new in 1996, are used on three routes: the 203 (Hounslow Bus Station-Staines Bus Station), 258 (Watford Junction-South Harrow Station) and 285 (Kingston-Heathrow Airport Central). Marshall-bodied SLFs can be found on routes 105 (Greenford-Heathrow Airport Central) and 490 (Richmond-Hatton Cross station).

The exceptions noted above are a trio of Renault S75s, required for the mobility routes, numbered 981-994. These are in a yellow and red livery, while the main fleet is similar, but with a brown skirt. The fleet of 60 vehicles is garaged at Bridge Road, Southall.

above: Dennis Dart DFD412/Plaxton Pointer 625 (N625 XJM), swings into the forecourt of Hatton Cross Station working a 285 (Kingston-Heathrow Airport Central) in March 1998.
Kevin Lane

right: DML653 (R653 TLM), a Marshall Capital-bodied Dennis Dart SLF, leaves Hatton Cross Station for Richmond in March 1998.
Kevin Lane

LONDON BUSLINES

LONDON CENTRAL

Top Left: A London Buslines Marshall-bodied Dennis Dart, R646 TLM, sits in the rain at Heathrow Airport before departing for Greenford on former CentreWest route 105, in March 1998. **Kevin Lane**

Bottom Left: London Central Volvo Olympian/Northern Counties NV71 (R271 LGH), negotiates the Elephant & Castle while on route 35 (Shoreditch High Street-Clapham Junction) in February 1998. **Kevin Lane**

Below: NV178 (R378 LGH) is one of the Northern Counties Palatine II-bodied Volvo Olympians put into service by London General on route 74 early in 1998. It is nosing into traffic in Baker Street at the start of its journey to Roehampton when new. **Kevin Lane**

LONDON GENERAL

Above: *All buses in the fleet are Dennis Darts, with the exception of three Renault-Dodge 18-seaters used on mobility routes 981-94. K651 DBL lays over at Brent Cross in January 1998.* **Kevin Lane**

London Central Bus Co Ltd

One Warner Road, Camberwell, London SE5 9LU

London Central, with garages at Camberwell, New Cross, Peckham and Bexleyheath, was bought by the Go-Ahead Group on 18 October 1994. Operations are thus not quite as central as its name may imply, as routes tend to spread southeast from the West End; indeed, Bexleyheath garage was formerly under Selkent control.

At privatisation, London Central's 498-strong fleet was dominated by two types: the Routemaster and Leyland Titan. Other double-deck classes represented were Optare Spectras (SP1/3-25) and 15 L class Leyland Olympians. MCW Metroriders were the most numerous single-deck type at 32, with Optare StarRiders (30) and Dennis Darts, bodied either by Plaxton or East Lancs (27), not far behind. Four Mercedes 811Ds were MTL1-4.

London Central still operates a predominantly double-deck fleet, with the Routemaster required for two routes: the 12 (Notting Hill Gate-Dulwich) and 36 (Queens Park Station-Lewisham). The 12 is worked by RMLs (Titans on Sunday), while the 36 has a mixed RM/RML allocation, with Titans and Olympians on Sundays. Of note is refurbished private hire RM9 at New Cross, one of the lowest bonnet numbers still in London, and pre-production RML883 at Camberwell.

Most of these Routemasters carry route-branding for either the 12 or 36. The RMLs are all powered by Cummins engines, while the RMs are being re-engined with Scania units.

By far the most numerous type is the Leyland Titan, represented at all four garages. Included is T1129, with coach-type seating and new to West Midlands PTE, and open-top T803, both at New Cross. Furthermore, a number of Titans are now used as driver trainers. T875 is a rest-room at Victoria for night-drivers, having replaced a former Portsmouth Leyland Atlantean. Other older double-deckers are a few Leyland Olympians — all at New Cross — and tend to work alongside Titans on routes with mixed allocations. L261 alone has coach seats. Another pre-privatisation class is represented by Volvo B10M-50/Northern Counties VC2, another coach-seated vehicle, acquired from London General in 1997.

Still in stock from privatisation are SP1/3-25 DAFSB250/Optare Spectras, unique in London, to be seen on route 3 (Oxford Circus-Crystal Palace) and some night routes also.

London Central was the first of the newly privatised former LBL companies to buy new double-deckers.

ve: London Central allocates Routemasters to routes 12 and 36; RM2151 (CUV 151C), appropriately *ded, stands at Victoria, Lewisham-bound in February 1998.* **Kevin Lane**

se are the NV class, Northern Counties-bodied
o Olympians. The first were delivered in March
5 and have currently reached NV88, thus allowing
and Titan withdrawals.
maller class of Volvo Olympians are the
ander-bodied AVs, nine of which were new in May
5 and are at Peckham for route P11 (Peckham-
ity Hall), currently shared with Titans.
gle-deckers are represented by seven classes,
of which are Dennis Darts. Oldest are the Plaxton-
ed DRL class — DRL1-16 — new in 1991 and all
ated to Bexleyheath garage for routes 178 and
. Also dating
1991 are
ht-bodied
4/51/55/56,

ht: The small
ch of DAF
are Spectras
ain on route 3
ord Circus-
stal Palace);
2 (K312 FYG)
otiates
algar Square,
ding south, in
ch 1998.
in Lane

ex-London General East Lancs-bodied DEL1-11 were
delivered shortly before privatisation and can usually
be found at Camberwell on route 484 (Camberwell
Green-Lewisham). The latest class of Darts are of the
low-floor SLF variety, Plaxton-bodied and designated
LDP. The first batch — LDP45-70 — went into service
in September 1997 from both Camberwell and New
Cross garages on route 345 (South Kensington-
Peckham), replacing Titans. Further deliveries of the
type followed for use on route 321 (New Cross Gate-
Foots Cray), LDP71-79/81-89 being supplied from
Bexleyheath and New Cross garages.

LONDON UNITED

LONDON SOVEREIGN

ove: Volvo Olympians with East Lancs Pyoneer bodywork work on Metrobus route 64 (New Addington-
ornton Heath Pond); R830 MFR, numerically the first of the batch of 15, was caught in West Croydon in March
98. **Kevin Lane**

o Left: London United operate Leyland Nationals on their H37 route from Hounslow to Richmond. Transferred
m Westlink and rebuilt to Urban Bus standards, they look a treat in the latest LU livery. LS153 (THX 153S)
ves the bus station and garage at Hounslow behind in this March 1998 view. **Kevin Lane**

ttom Left: London Sovereign generally use Northern Counties-bodied Leyland Olympians on route 114 (Mill
Broadway Station-Ruislip Station). One such, L147 (H147 GGS), loads at Harrow-on-the-Hill in January 1998,
front of a London United Olympian on route 140. **Kevin Lane**

The other three classes of single-deckers are all midibuses: Optare StarRiders of class SR are now at Camberwell for routes P5 but are due for early withdrawal, while MetroRiders are allocated to Bexleyheath for several local routes and at Peckham for routes P12, P13 and S12. The latter were acquired from London General early in 1998 and replaced Peckham's StarRiders. Alexander-bodied Mercedes-Benz 811Ds of the MA class, acquired from London General in 1996/7, act as spare vehicles at Camberwell for routes 484 and P5.

Above: *The Leyland Titan is the most numerous class of double-decker in the London Central fleet. T1016 (A616 THV) works a 45 from Kings Cross Station to Brixton Hill along Farringdon Street in March 1998.* **Kevin Lane**

Below: *LDP45-89 are Dennis Dart SLFs with Plaxton Pointer 36-seat bodies, delivered during 1997. LDP67 (R467 LGH) turns outside of the Arding & Hobbs department store at Clapham Junction on route 345 (Peckham– South Kensington), previously operated by Titans, in March 1998.* **Kevin Lane**

Above: Earlier Darts include the 21-strong DRL-class, also with Plaxton Pointer bodies, dating from 1991. DRL7 (J607 XHL) is in Woolwich on the 178 to Kidbrooke in April 1998. **Kevin Lane**

Below: Also in Woolwich, with the ferry and the River Thames behind, is MRL157 (H157 UUA), one of a number of Optare MetroRiders in the fleet. It is on local route 291 in April 1998. **Kevin Lane**

MTL LONDON

SELKENT

ove: *The majority of the Metroline single-deck fleet are Dennis Darts of one sort or another. The 32 dual-door axton Pointer-bodied SLFs, DLD22-53, entered service during 1997, including DLD32 at Brent Cross in nuary 1998, having arrived from Kilburn Park station. Alongside is Arriva The Shires Olympian 5112 (G282 MJ) about to work back to Watford Junction.* **Kevin Lane**

p Left: *MTL London has Routemasters scheduled for one route, the 10, from Archway to Hammersmith oadway. RM1799 (799 DYE), proceeds along Caledonian Road in March 1998.* **Kevin Lane**

ottom Left: *Widmore Road, Bromley is the setting for two Selkent types; Leyland Titan T1108 (B108 WUV) is ssed by Dennis Lance/Plaxton Verde LV6 (L206 YAG) on routes 162 and 227 respectively. A Capital Logistics AF heads towards Dartford in this rather damp April 1998 view.* **Kevin Lane**

London General Transport Services Ltd

25 Raleigh Gardens, Mitcham, Surrey CR4 3AB

London General, the largest of the LBL fleets at 639 buses, was sold to its management on 3 October 1994. Its operating area is southwest London, with garages at Waterloo, Battersea, Merton, Putney, Stockwell and Sutton, and among its responsibilities are the various Red Arrow routes on which Leyland National 2s converted to National Greenway specification are used.

The opening fleet contained a large number of Metrobuses, with Routemasters and Volvos making up the double-deck fleet. Single-deckers were various types of Dennis Darts, Volvo B10Bs, the aforementioned National Greenways (including several un-rebuilt Leyland National 2s) and a number of Mercedes and MetroRider midibuses of classes MA, MRL and MT.

The Metrobus still occupies the position of being the largest class, M11 being the lowest numbered. Of note are two open-top examples, numbered OM171 and OM241, both of which carry 'General' red and white livery, applied in prewar style. Closed-top M1432 and M1440 have been similarly treated. The

Routemaster fleet, of 69 vehicles, has remained constant since privatisation. With the exception of RM994, all are Iveco-engined RMLs and include pre-production RML887/889/894/899. RML2516 has bee fitted with platform doors and is now classified DRM. The Routemasters are allocated to Waterloo and Putney garages for route 11 (Liverpool Street station-Fulham Broadway), route 14 (Tottenham Court Road Station-Putney Heath) and route 22 (Putney Common Piccadilly Circus).

The Volvo double-deckers in stock at privatisation were VC1-39, Northern Counties-bodied Citybus B10Ms, delivered in 1989-91. Except for VC39, which arrived in December 1991, the others were bought in two batches: VC1-27 for route 133 (Liverpool Street Station-Tooting Broadway), and VC28-38 for route 19 (Norwood Junction-Brixton), the latter subsequently lost to London Central. They still perform on the 133, the spare vehicles turning up on other Stockwell routes. VC1 and VC3 have coach seating (as does VC3 transferred to London Central in February 1997). VC1 is at Sutton, where it is available for school and

Below: The impressive bulk of NV178 (R378 LGH), one of the Volvo Olympians with Northern Counties Palatine bodywork, introduced onto the 74 (Baker Street-Roehampton) during January 1998. It is seen after being in service for only a month, caught in traffic in Baker Street at the start of its long journey south. **Kevin Lane**

vate hire duties. A number of the class now carry registrations of former Routemasters.

he new generation of double-deckers are Volvo mpians with Northern Counties Palatine bodywork the NV class. Deliveries began early in 1997 with 101-115, and ended with NV147-159 a year or so er. They are currently allocated to Sutton and tney garages and have replaced Metrobuses. 161-187 were delivered in late 1997/early 1998 d have dual purpose-seated Northern Counties atine II bodywork. They ousted Metrobuses on te 74 (Baker Street-Roehampton).

lost of the single-deck fleet consists of the vitable Dennis Dart, in various forms. The oldest the DWs, Wright-bodied examples dating from 90-3, 28 of which were in stock at privatisation and ich are still in stock. They work from Sutton and rton garages. Other Darts in stock in October 1994

were a number of Plaxton Pointer-bodied members of the DR and DRL classes, represented at all garages except Sutton and Waterloo. Two classes of Dart have been added to the London General fleet since 1994; DPL and LDP. DPL1-16 are also Plaxton Pointer-bodied Darts, but have a higher seating capacity (35) than the DR/DRL classes, which variously seat 28, 32 or 34. All 16 are at Merton garage for routes 200 (Raynes Park-Mitcham) and 201 (Mitcham-Tulse Hill). The LDP class are low-floor SLFs, again carrying Plaxton Pointer bodies. LDP1-17 seat 32, while longer LDP18-44 seat 36. Their allocation is split between Sutton (19) and Merton (25). In a class all of its own is VWL1, a Wright Crusader-bodied Volvo B6LE, new in 1995. Registered N101 HGO, it has now been allocated to Surrey County Council 'Access Bus' routes. One coach is owned, TPL10, a 1986 Plaxton-bodied Leyland Tiger, currently on loan to Nostalgiabus.

Above: Waterloo station is the setting for GLS500 (GUW 500W), one of the Leyland National 2s rebuilt to Greenway standards by East Lancs. They are used on Red Arrow services, in this case the 507 to Victoria station. **Kevin Lane**

Before moving onto the midibuses, it should be noted that the entire class of Volvo B10Bs, the VN class totalling 13 vehicles and new in 1993, was transferred to Oxford during 1997. They were used on route 88 (Clapham Common-Oxford Circus), but were eventually removed due to problems with long rear overhangs. Metrobuses now work the route.

The active midibus fleet is now down to two classes following the withdrawal of the MA class of Mercedes. A handful of long MetroRiders, MRLs, are in stock, while ML1-15 are 29-seat Marshall Minibuses, new in

1996/7. These numbers are currently depleted with the loan of ML1-6 to Limebourne for use on route C2 on which they formerly ran for London General. The others are at Putney, seeing use on routes 39 and 265. A Freight Rover Sherpa, SC1, is used for driver training.

Below: LDP8 (188 CLT), a 1996 Dennis Dart SLF/Plaxton Pointer, approaching Sutton station on route 80 (Hackbridge-Belmont) in March 1998. **Kevin Lane**

Left: Wright-bodied Dennis Dart DW128 (K128 LGO), one of 24 in the fleet, at Clapham Junction working a 170 towards Roehampton in March 1998.
Kevin Lane

London Sovereign

ation Road, Borehamwood, Hertfordshire, WD6 1HB

ndon Sovereign, formerly known as BTS Coaches, s been part of Blazefield Holdings since August 94. As BTS, it began operating LT route 292 orehamwood-Edgware Station) in February 1988, ing over from London Country North East on an ergency basis due to industrial action. The route osequently passed to BTS, who operated it until it s lost to Metroline. The 114 (Mill Hill Broadway-islip), was gained from January 1991 and is still erated today. Perhaps its most noteworthy eration is that of the 13 (Golders Green Station-dwych), won in 1993. RMLs, leased from London

Regional Transport, are used Monday to Saturday, with Olympians on Sundays. The Olympians, Northern Counties-bodied and new in 1991, are also found daily on the 114, the route for which they were bought. Five ex-London Leyland Titans are also in the fleet, used on school route 606 and as spare vehicles to the Olympians. Hertfordshire County Council school route 861 (Borehamwood Station-Townsend School) is also worked.

Livery is poppy red with yellow and the depot is next to Elstree & Borehamwood station, in Station Road.

ght: The only utemasters w to reach olders Green are e poppy red es operated by ndon Sovereign their route 13 Aldwych. ML2538 ID 538D) oceeds along chley Road rough Childs l in January 98.
vin Lane

London United Busways Ltd
Busways House, Wellington Road, Fulwell, Middlesex, TW2 5NT

Stanwell Buses Ltd
6 Pulborough Way, Hounslow, Middlesex, TW4 6DE

London United was sold to its management on 5 November 1994, the deal including 465 vehicles and garages at Fulwell, Hounslow, Shepherds Bush and Stamford Brook. Stanwell Buses, trading as Westlink, was acquired from West Midlands Travel in September 1995.

Stanwell Buses, trading as Westlink, had been set up in 1986 as a subsidiary of London Buses, initially to work Surrey County Council-tendered services, although operations were subsequently expanded to include LRT tenders also. Stanwell was privatised in January 1994, the first London Buses subsidiary to do so, sold initially to its management but passing to West Midlands Travel after only three months.

London United's operating territory extends from central London westwards to Hammersmith, Hounslow, Heathrow, Richmond, Kingston and into Surrey; indeed several routes are wholly in Surrey. Trunk routes include the 27 (Turnham Green-Camden Town), 94 (Acton Green-Piccadilly Circus) and night route N97 (Trafalgar Square-Heathrow). London United is also responsible for the airbus services — A1 and

A2 — connecting Heathrow with Victoria and King's Cross respectively. The Westlink operations are conducted from bases at Kingston and Hounslow Heath. The majority of Westlink's routes fall outside the LT network, being either commercial, or under contract to Surrey County Council.

The initial London United fleet was very much double-deck orientated: RMLs and Metrobuses were in the majority, with Airbus-dedicated vehicles amongst the latter type. Other double-deckers were a batch of Leyland Olympians (L292-314). Single-deck types showed a little more variety, with a number of Dennis Dart variants, 10 Dennis Lance SLFs and half a-dozen Leyland Lynxes. In conclusion, there were also eight Iveco 49.10s and four MetroRiders.

Today, Routemasters are confined to two routes: the 9 (Hammersmith-Aldwych) and 94 (Acton Green-Piccadilly), both only Mondays to Saturdays of course, with Metrobuses on Sundays. Except for two RMs — 2033/2078 — all are Cummins-engined RMLs and include pre-production RML880/881/891. RML880 carries a prewar traditional livery and is numbered

Above: Routemasters are now only scheduled for routes 9 and 94; RML 2293 (CUV 293C) heads through Shepherds Bush on a Piccadilly Circus-bound 94 in March 1998. **Kevin Lane**

M880. They are allocated to Shepherds Bush garage. Metrobuses are still in the majority and are presented at all garages. A few are now dedicated driver training buses. The Airbus Metrobuses were superseded in 1995/6 by a new generation of vehicles on these services. These are Volvo Olympians with Alexander Royale bodywork, numbered (but not carried) A112-130. The need for generous luggage space and the desire for many passengers to sit downstairs has resulted in the unusual seating configuration of 43 over 9.

Leyland-bodied Leyland Olympians L292-314, new in 1989, are still in the fleet. Allocated to Hounslow garage, most can be found on route 140 (Heathrow Airport-Harrow Weald), with a number being route-branded as such. Others, including coach-seated L12-4, are used as spare vehicles to Metrobuses, so can turn up on other routes also. Other Olympians are 10 Volvos with Alexander Royale bodywork, new in 1996 and numbered VA1-10. They are scheduled for route 131 (Wimbledon-Kingston), formerly operated by Westlink with Leyland Titans.

The London United single-deck fleet is mainly composed of Dennis Darts. Large numbers of DR and DRL classes, bodied by Reeve Burgess and Plaxton, and DT class, with bodywork by Duple and Carlyle, are in stock. Some of the DR and DRLs carry a dedicated livery for route 555 (Walton on Thames-Heathrow). Also in a dedicated livery were a number of dual-purpose seated DTs used on 'Airbus Direct' duties, linking Heathrow with various hotels in central London, although some have now been downgraded to bus use. The latest Darts date from 1996: Wright-bodied CD1-8, on route H25 (Hatton Cross station-Hanworth).

Perhaps the most notable of the single-deckers is the LS class of Leyland Nationals, dating from 1977/9, scheduled for route H37 (Hounslow Bus station-Richmond station). Along with those with Westlink, these are the last of the breed with the former London bus units (those with London General are of course Greenway rebuilds of Leyland National 2s). Despite their years, these refurbished vehicles look well in the latest London United livery. Working alongside the LSs at Hounslow are six Leyland Lynxes (LX3-8), new in 1989.

Other single-deckers are LLW1-10. These are low-floor Wright-bodied Dennis Lances, new in 1993/4 for route 120 (Hounslow Bus Station-Northolt).

Westlink today is quite an interesting little fleet. The only double-deck route is the 57 (Kingston-Streatham Hill), the recipient of new Volvo Olympians with Alexander (Belfast) bodies, which replaced Metrobuses at the end of 1997. They are numbered VA11-31 and currently carry a mixture of Irish and UK 'R' registrations.

Above: Airbus routes A1 and A2 use Alexander Royale-bodied Volvo Olympians, quite an improvement on the Metrobuses used hitherto. A126 (N126 YRW) leaves King's Cross in January 1998. **Kevin Lane**

The oldest of the single-deckers are a number of LS class Leyland Nationals, dating variously between 1976-9 and are used on a number of routes, mainly from Hounslow Heath. LS227 carries a mainly white livery for Kingston University contracts and is fitted with a wheelchair lift. DA1-9 are DAF Optare Deltas dating from 1989/90 and are common on route 81 (Hounslow-Slough). MAN Optare Vectas are numbered MV1-8 and these are scheduled on route 371 (Kingston-Richmond) alongside Optare Excels XL1-6, both types being branded as such.

Two Dennis Dart classes are operating with Westlink: DR and DWL. The DRs have Reeve Burgess and Plaxton Pointer bodies and were transferred from

London United, mainly during 1996, while DWL1-14 are bodied by Wright. DWL1-3 also carry Kingston University white contract livery. A final vehicle in this livery is former demonstrator Metrorider MR134, one of a number of this type that have recently spent periods in store. Three, numbered MRW2-4 and re-registered A2-4 LBR (London Borough of Richmond) 1996 are fitted for chair-lifts and now see use on route H20 (Hounslow-Ivybridge Estate). There is also the last surviving FS-class Ford Transit — FS29 — at Hounslow Heath.

London United has relieved its basic red livery with white roof area and grey skirt, while Westlink vehicles are red with grey.

Above: A few Leyland Olympians are used as spare vehicles at Hounslow. Leyland-bodied L313 (G313 UYK) is seen here at the bus station covering for an LLW-class Dennis Lance on route 120 to Southall in March 1998. **Kevin Lane**

Left: Kingston is the setting for Westlink VA21 (R921 WOE), leaving for Streatham Hill on route 57 in March 1998. These Alexander (Belfast)-bodied Volvo Olympians were introduced onto this service from the previous December, ousting Metrobuses. **Kevin Lane**

above: Westlink's DAF Optare Deltas are common on the 81 (Hounslow-Slough) as illustrated by DA1 (carrying third registration F802 NGY), in Hounslow in March 1998.
Kevin Lane

above: Five Westlink buses carry a white livery for contracts for Kingston University, including Wright-bodied Dennis Darts, DWL1-3. DWL2 (JDZ 2402) arrives in Surbiton to meet a train at the station in March 1998.
Kevin Lane

Metrobus Ltd

Oak Farm, Farnborough Hill, Orpington, Kent, BR6 6DA

Metrobus was formed by Tillingbourne (Metropolitan) Ltd, a subsidiary company of Tillingbourne, the long-established Surrey independent, to run its services in the Croydon and Orpington areas, taking effect from September 1983. LT-tendered work came its way in August 1986, gaining operation of routes 61 and 361. Its original routes in the Croydon area also became part of the LT-tendered network, but have since become commercial services (353/354) or have been withdrawn (357). In June 1997, Metrobus bought East Surrey Buses, amounting to some 26 routes in Surrey and Kent and 23 vehicles. The former Leisurelink operations in East Sussex were fully taken over in July 1997, trading as Metrobus South Coast. Both these and the former East Surrey operations are, of course, outside the scope of this book.

As far as London is concerned, LRT routes 64, 138, 146, 161, 181, 233, 261, 284 and school routes 630 and 693 are operated, while 351-4, 356, 358, 361 and 654 are commercial routes in the Bromley/Croydon areas. Also noteworthy is commuter route 705 into London and several Sunday routes to the coast. The late summer of

1998 will see Metrobus also working tendered routes 119 and 320, which will require more Volvo Olympians. Furthermore, Darts will be needed for new commercial route 446 at the same time.

In the early days, the fleet featured many second-hand double-deckers, including the ubiquitous DMS. Today, a more modern image is presented; MetroRiders are used on the 138, while a selection of Plaxton Pointer-bodied Dennis Darts, including a batch from Kentish Bus, are used on routes 146, 161 (Sundays), 284, 351, 352, 353/354 (Sundays) and 361, and a number of ECW-bodied Leyland Olympians. Low-floor Darts are specified for the 181 and 233. Other single-deck routes are the 354/356, using Leyland Lynxes, both new and second-hand, and the 358, which requires low-floor Optare Excels.

Double-deckers now in the fleet for London service are Leyland-bodied Leyland Olympians on routes 161, 353 354 and one with ECW bodywork used on school duties. Volvo Olympians with Northern Counties Palatine bodies are to be found on the 261, while East Lancs Pyoneer

bodywork is carried by the Volvo Olympians on route 64. (Perhaps inappropriately, no MCW Metrobuses are scheduled for operation in London, although a number are used in Sussex. A few did turn up on the 261 pending the arrival of new Olympians, however.)

Metrobus livery is blue and yellow and the London operations are conducted from the Farnborough Hill depot at Green Street Green, near Orpington.

Above: East Lancs Pyoneer-bodied Volvo Olympian R835 MFR, caught in the spring sunshine at West Croydon in March 1998. It is working on route 64 (Thornton Heath Pond-New Addington), won from South London in August 1997. **Kevin Lane**

Right: Eleven Northern Counties Palatine I-bodied Volvo Olympians, 817-829, were new in 1996. No 828 (P828 SGP), proceeds down Bromley High Street towards Bromley Common having begun its journey in Lewisham. **Kevin Lane**

Left: Four Plaxton Pointer-bodied Dennis Dart SLFs entered the fleet early in 1998, Nos 741-745. No 743 (R743 BMY) picks up at Catford on route 181 (Lewisham-Downham) in April 1998. Kevin Lane

Right: Nos 501-510 are Optare Excels; 505 (P505 OUG) heads towards Orpington station on route 358 from Crystal Palace in April 1998. Kevin Lane

Left: Among the older single-deckers are a trio of Leyland Lynx that originated with Merthyr Tydfil in 1987. No 103 (D103 NDW) swings into Wellesley Road, East Croydon, arriving from Bromley North on route 354 in April 1998. Kevin Lane

Right: MetroRider H152 UUA, formerly Selkent MRL152, acquired by Metrobus in January 1998. It is waiting to leave for Coney Hall on route 138 in April 1998. Kevin Lane

Metroline Travel Ltd

118-122 College Road, Harrow, Middlesex, HA1 1DB

Metroline, operating in northwest London, was privatised on 7 October 1994, passing to its management. An early acquisition was that of Atlas Bus & Coach, bought from its owners, London Coaches, on 28 November 1994. By the time of its takeover by Metroline, Atlas was running only on route 52/N52, using ex-LBL Leyland Titans. The two initial Atlas routes — the 107 and 112 — had earlier been re-tendered to Metroline, although the latter subsequently passed to MTL London. The Brents Travel Group also passed to Metroline, on 10 October 1995, bringing with it a base in Watford and a fleet of 30 coaches. This site has now closed in preference of the former Atlas Bus depot in Harlesden. Metroline currently operates from garages at Willesden, Edgware, Harrow Weald, North Wembley and Cricklewood.

Routemasters are allocated to Willesden for routes 6 (Kensal Rise Station-Aldwych) and 98 (Willesden Garage-Holborn) both Mondays to Saturdays, with Metrobuses used evenings and Sundays. RMLs are used, including pre-production RML893/902, while other Routemasters include RM70, open-top RM644 and traditionally liveried RMC1513.

Alexander-bodied Volvo Olympians are to be seen on routes 52/N52, having been delivered during late 1996

to replace the Leyland Titans that came from London Coaches. A few of the latter survive, however, in the Contract Services fleet. Most of the double-deckers are MCW Metrobuses, around 170 of them, allocated to a garages except North Wembley. A number are also pa of the Contract fleet, whose responsibilities include schools, free supermarket buses, private hire and other special duties. Notable are the first five London Metrobuses, M1-5, now used for driver training.

Dennis Darts form the bulk of the single-deck fleet, more so since the early withdrawal of the LN class of Dennis Lances. The Reeve Burgess Pointer and Plaxto Pointer-bodied DR class are in use with the diminishing Carlyle-bodied DT class, together with the longer EDR class. Route 186 (Northwick Park Hospital Brent Cross shopping centre) requires low-floor Denni Lance SLFs (Wright-bodied LLW25-38), mostly delivered in 1994, while newer low-floor buses are Dennis Dart SLFs with Plaxton bodies, of classes DL, DLS and DLD, the latter having dual-doors. These types can be found on routes 90 (DL), 204, 206 (DLS) and 189, 316 (DLS). Further DL/DLDs are on order. Th coaches in the Brent operation include Mercedes, Volvo, DAF and Dennis types.

The red livery of Metrobus is relieved by a dark blue skirt, while Brents coaches are white.

Above: The newest double-deckers to date are AV1-22, Alexander-bodied Volvo Olympians, now approaching two years old. They are allocated to Willesden garage for routes 52/N52 to Victoria. AV16 (P476 MBY) nears its destination of Victoria in January 1998. **Kevin Lane**

Above: The Monday to Friday requirement for route 6 is 22 RMLs; RML2274 (CUV 274C) heads back to Willesden along The Strand in March 1998. **Kevin Lane**

Left: A number of Metrobuses feature in the Contract Services fleet, including M429 (GYE 429W). On this occasion it is seen in Garston, having just passed the Shires garage, working schools service 833 (Garston, St Michaels RC School-South Oxhey), one of several routes operated under contract to Hertfordshire County Council. The picture was taken in October 1997, from the top deck of a passing Shires Olympian.
Kevin Lane

Right: Dennis Lance SLFs with Wright bodywork can be found on route 186; LW32 (L32 WLH) turns into Greenhill Way, Harrow in January 1998.
Kevin Lane

Above: *The majority of Metroline single-deckers are Dennis Darts. New in 1994 were Plaxton Pointer-bodied EDR1-9, of which EDR5 (M105 BLE) was at Edgware on a Queensbury-bound 288 in October 1997.* **Kevin Lan**

Below: *The earliest Darts date from 1990/91; Carlyle-bodied DT103 (H103 MOB) wears a dark blue livery and operates a courtesy service for Tescos at Brent Cross as seen here in January 1998.* **Kevin Lane**

MTL London Northern Ltd

I House, 17-19 Highgate Hill, London N19 5NA

verpool-based MTL Trust Holdings was the
ccessful bidder for London Northern, the acquisition
king place on 26 October 1994. London Northern,
th 340 vehicles, operated from central London out
Hertfordshire, via the north London suburbs. It
cluded a garage, still operated, in Potters Bar, well
tside the Greater London boundary in Hertfordshire.
he fleet at takeover contained a number of varied
pes. Double-deckers were principally Routemasters
d Metrobuses, with a small batch of Scanias for
od measure. Two Ailsas and two Daimler Fleetlines,
e a trainer, the other open-top, completed the
cture. There were also two classes of Dennis Darts
d a number of MCW and Mercedes midibuses,
gether with a quartet of de-licensed LS class
yland Nationals. Two coaches were also owned: a
lvo B10M and, more impressively, a Neoplan
kyliner double-deck coach, appropriately registered
KY 1.

Changes were soon apparent, including a move of
eadquarters from expensive WC1 to more reasonable
9. Within a few months, expansion was in the air,
th the acquisition by MTL of another Liverpool-based
mpany, Gemsam Holdings in April 1995. Trading as

London Suburban Buses, Gemsam had won four LT
tenders, ironically at the expense of the old London
Northern. A total of 51 buses were taken-over, mainly
ex-London Leyland Titans, but including a batch of two-
year-old Olympians.

A second acquisition in London took place in October
of the same year, when R&I Tours of Park Royal came
under MTL ownership. Six LT tenders were operated
and 39 buses and 25 coaches were in the fleet. The
coaches were integrated with those of MTL under the
SightseerS name. At about this time the 'Northern' part
of the title was dropped; with a new base in west
London; this was no doubt seen as inappropriate should
further expansion in this area arise. The R&I operations
were initially run as a separate unit, although they were
subsequently absorbed into the main fleet. The
SightseerS operation was wound up in 1997, many of
the coaches being sold in the August.

Four classes of double-deckers are currently operated,
although no new vehicles have been bought since the
MTL takeover. Routemasters are now scheduled only for
one route following the conversion of the 139 to SLF
Darts in March 1998.This last route is the 10
(Hammersmith-King's Cross Station), requiring just 19

*bove: MTL has only route 10 scheduled for Routemaster operation. Pre-production RML903 (WLT 903) heads
or Hammersmith at Kings Cross in February 1998. **Kevin Lane***

Above: The former London Suburban Bus Volvo Olympians are numbered V201-17 and feature Merseyside registrations. V201 (L201 SKD) heads for Liverpool Street at Archway in April 1998 on route 271, despite the blind display! *Kevin Lane*

RMLs from Mondays to Saturdays. Metrobuses make up the majority of double-deckers, all allocated to Holloway and Potters Bar garages.

Ten Alexander-bodied Scania N112DRBs are currently in stock, allocated to Potters Bar and numbered S11-20. These are now in fleet livery following the withdrawal of the X43 'Red Express' route. They are used on the 84 (St Alban's City station-New Barnet station), on which they had previously turned up at weekends. The class

formerly included S1-10/21, used on route 263, although these went north to MTL Liverpool following the loss of the contract to Leaside in 1996.

The newest double-deckers are 16 Volvo Olympians (V201-10/12-17) with Northern Counties Palatine II dual-door bodywork. Their Merseyside registrations indicate that they were acquired with the takeover of London Suburban Buses in 1995 and were new in 1993/4. Allocated to Holloway garage, they are normal...

Below: The most numerous double-deck class are MCW Metrobuses, with over 180 in stock. M161 (BYX 161V) heads towards New Barnet station on an 84 in St Albans in October 1997, a route since converted to S-class Scania operation. *Kevin Lane*

Above: A number of Marshall-bodied MAN single-deckers entered the fleet in 1996, including MM272 (P472 JEG) seen loading at Edgware for Alperton on route 79 in November 1997. Ten years earlier, the route had been put out to tender, being won by London Buslines. **Kevin Lane**

be seen on routes W7 (Finsbury Park Station-Muswell Hill Broadway), shared with Metrobuses, and 271 (Highgate Village-Liverpool Street Station).

There is rather more variety in the single-deck fleet, by virtue of the R&I takeover. The Dennis Dart is well represented, as elsewhere, with six classes: DNL, DRL, DC, DM, DP and DT. DNL101-10/12-120 were delivered shortly before privatisation, in May and June 1994, carrying Northern Counties Paladin 34-seat bodywork. They still work on the route for which they were bought, the C2 'CamdenLink' (Parliament Hill Fields-Oxford Circus), on which they replaced Optare StarRiders.

The DRLs date from 1992 and carry 34-seat Plaxton Pointer bodywork, being numbered DRL18-37. Their

Left: DC220 (G220 LGK) is one of a number of Dennis Darts from the R&I fleet. New in 1990 it carries a Duple/Carlyle Dartline body and is in Golders Green, arriving on a 268 from Finchley Road Station in January 1998. **Kevin Lane**

Above: Dual doored Marshall-bodied Dennis Dart SLFs took over from Routemasters on route 139 from 28 March 1998. On the following day, a Sunday, DML14 (R694 MEW) is seen at the end of its journey, Trafalgar Square. **Philip Wallis**

usual haunts are currently routes C11/C12 and 274, the former operated by R&I, although those on the C11/12 are due to be replaced during 1998.

Two classes of Dennis Dart were acquired with R&I

Tours, DC216/19-21/24/29/32 and DP233-41/45-48. The DCs carry Duple Dartline 36-seat bodies (excepting DC232, a Carlyle body), and were new in 1990, while the DP class have Plaxton Pointer bodies, seating either

Above: OM244 (M502 ALP) is one of a pair of Optare MetroRiders bought for R&I Tours in 1996. Although apparently more usual on the H2, it is seen here at Golders Green working on an H3 in January 1998. **Kevin Lane**

5 or 40, and were new in 1992-5. The DP class was rther extended in 1997 with the addition of DP273-76. ue DC and DP classes work from the former R&I base North Acton on routes 46 and 112, while the four ewer DPs are at Holloway working alongside DRLs on ute 274.

The six members of the DT class were acquired in ecember 1996 from Metroline following a period on an. These carry Carlyle 28-seat bodywork and were ew in 1990. The lone DM242 carries 40-seat Marshall odywork and was acquired from Ryan, Langridge, in une 1996. Further second-hand Darts entered the fleet February 1998 with the loan of the 17 from hamesway used on route 214 (Highgate Village-verpool Street station), pending the arrival of new uses.

Marshall-bodied Dennis Darts of two classes appeared the fleet early in 1998: single-door SLFs, classified MS, were for route 234 (Potters Bar Garage-Muswell ill Broadway), while dual-door SLFs, DML class, went route 139 (West End Lane-Trafalgar Square). Optare tarRiders and Routemasters were replaced espectively.

There are several other single-deck types to note. A io of DAF SB220s is at Potters Bar for route 310A Enfield Town-Hertford), operated jointly with Arriva East erts & Essex (formerly County Bus). Two are Optare eltas, while the third has Ikarus Citibus bodywork. Two

classes of MAN single-deckers are now in stock: 1995 saw the entry into service of Optare Vectas with R&I Tours, duly becoming MV249-53 with MTL, while Marshall-bodied MANs are MM254-68 and 270-78. The first batch was bought for R&I, while the second was new to MTL. All are at North Acton, scheduled for routes 79 and 95.

Mercedes-Benz Optare StarRiders are SR108-117/20/21. All are at Potters Bar garage for route 234 from Muswell Hill Broadway, shared with another class, the MW, Wright-bodied Mercedes-Benz. These are also seen on Potters Bar routes 326, 384 and 385 as well as a free bus service for the local Tesco supermarket. Both classes pre-date privatisation as do Optare MetroRiders MRL210-22, although two further examples were added in 1997 as MRL223/4. These vehicles are at Potters Bar and Holloway for routes W4 and W5 respectively. Three other Optare MetroRiders are OM243/4/79, the first two coming from R&I Tours, and can usually be found on Hampstead Garden Suburb route H2. Routes H1/H3, worked in conjunction with the H2, are the preserve of MMS269, a 26-seat Marshall-bodied Mercedes-Benz 811D. All three are best observed at Golders Green station. Another 'one off' in the fleet is Potters Bar's Marshall Minibus (actually a 29-seater), used on local route PB1. Several miscellaneous vehicles to note are MR87/90, Mercedes-Benz/Robin Hood midicoaches and a trio of Iveco Daily 49.10 minibuses.

Below: Other Optare MetroRiders in the fleet, include 15 for routes W4/W5; MRL218 (J218 BWU) passes hrough Turnpike Lane on route W4 in April 1998. **Kevin Lane**

Nostalgiabus Ltd

Unit 2, Abbey Industrial Estate, 24 Willow Lane, Mitcham, Surrey

Nostalgiabus came to prominence with the introduction of a half-hourly Monday to Saturday route between Epsom and Kingston in December 1997. The 306 was born out of a reduction by London & Country on its 406 between the two towns. Routemasters are generally used on the service, and are of course crew-worked. Nostalgiabus is also involved in school and contract work on which a variety of vintage and more modern vehicles are employed. An ex-London GS and RF are in stock, together with several Olympians, a 1977 AEC Reliance and a Leyland Tiger on loan from London General. Livery is generally red and cream.

Above: *It is a few years since the last London Routemaster ran in Kingston, so those of Nostalgiabus on their 306 limited stop service from Epsom are a welcome sight. Former RM1394 (394 CLT) sets off from Eden Street in March 1998.* **Kevin Lane**

Sovereign Buses (Harrow) Ltd

Babbage Road, Stevenage, Hertfordshire, SG1 2EQ

Part of Blazefield Holdings, Sovereign Buses (Harrow) was created in 1990 to operate local services won in the Harrow area, starting in December of that year. These routes were numbered H10, H11, H13 and H17 and are still operated today, using Mercedes midibuses. In addition, the 398 (Ruislip-Islip Manor Estate), latterly worked by Blue & White Buses, is now worked by Sovereign Buses (Harrow), having been initially worked on a temporary basis since early 1997.

Buses carry a blue and cream livery and are garaged at the premises of Venture Transport, Harrow.

above: The entire Sovereign Harrow fleet is made up of Mercedes midibuses, based either on their 709D or 811D models. No 409 (H409 FGS) is one of the latter and carries Reeve Burgess 31-seat bodywork. It is pictured in Harrow-on-the-Hill working on route H17, Harrow Bus Station to Vale Farm Sports Centre in January 1998. **Kevin Lane**

South East London & Kent Bus Co Ltd (Selkent)

80 Bromley Road, Catford, London, SE6 2XA

Above: The next Volvo Olympians, also Northern Counties-bodied, were delivered in 1997/98 and received class prefixes to their fleetnumbers, VN82-110. VN107 (R107 XNO) and VN88 (R188 XNO) are in Wellington Street, Woolwich, both working towards Plumstead Garage on route 54 from West Croydon in April 1998. **Kevin Lane**

Selkent was the other former London Buses company to be bought by Stagecoach Holdings plc. On 6 September 1994 it was acquired along with East London. As its official title implies, Stagecoach Selkent's operations are based in southeast London towards Kent, and have three garages, in Plumstead, Bromley and Catford. Several trunk routes are run into central London, including the 53 (Oxford Circus-Plumstead station) and the 185 (Victoria station-Lewisham).

Its opening fleet totalled 414 vehicles, offering quite a variety of types. Alone among the fleets privatised in 1994/5, Selkent did not have any routes operated by the Routemaster. Double-deckers available for service were confined to Titans and Olympians, while single-deck types were more numerous, including Dennis Darts and Lances, MetroRiders, Ivecos and several classes of Mercedes. In addition, eight DAF coaches were also in stock.

The 1998 fleet contains rather fewer classes, particularly amongst the midibuses. Leyland Titans and Olympians are still the dominant double-deck types, the new classes both being Volvo Olympians. The Leyland Olympians all carry ECW bodies and date from 1986, the lowest number being L7. They work routes from Plumstead and Catford garages. Of note are the last three — L260/262/263 — all of which have coach-type seating. These, along with L91, have been re-registered. The Leyland Titans date from 1979-84 and work from Bromley and Catford garages. T86/98/114/120/130/137/142 and 224 are dedicated to driver training duties and carry the Stagecoach corporate stripes on white livery.

The first new double-deckers under Stagecoach ownership were Volvo Olympians with Northern Counties Palatine I bodies, delivered during the summer and autumn of 1995 for service at Plumstead. These did not receive a class prefix, being numbered simply 301-352. The other new double-deckers to date are also Volvo Olympians with Northern Counties bodywork, although these carry VN prefixes to their numbers (VN82-110). They were delivered in 1997/8 for routes 54 at Plumstead and 75 at Catford, resulting in the cascading of L class Olympians and the withdrawal of Titans.

Dennis Darts form several classes, the oldest being the Carlyle-bodied DTs and the Wright-bodied DWs, dating from 1990 and 1991 respectively. Most are at Catford, the DWs being found on the P4 (Brixton Station-Lewisham). The most numerous type are the

Previous page: Volvo Olympians with Northern Counties bodywork first entered the fleet in 1995. No 304 (M304 DGP) was among the first, and one of their duties is route P3 (London Bridge-New Cross Gate) on which it is seen, at London Bridge, in February 1998. **Kevin Lane**

Above: Just over 100 Leyland Titans feature in this double-deck dominated fleet. T560 (NUW 560Y) is Leyland-bodied and is drawing to a stop at East Croydon station on route 194 (West Croydon-Forest Hill) in March 1998. *Kevin Lane*

Below: The Alexander Dash-bodied Dennis Darts are numbered 601-40, with no class prefix. No 639 (P639 PGP) is running between Peckham and Abbey Wood Station on route 177 at Woolwich in April 1998. *Kevin Lane*

85

Alexander-bodied Darts (numbered 601-640, no class prefix is carried) delivered during 1995/6. Five further DWs came from East London in February 1998, along with five Plaxton-bodied DRLs, while PDs from Stagecoach Oxford are also arriving in the fleet.

Low-floor Darts are Alexander-bodied SLD20-29, which entered service at Bromley late in 1997 on route 314 (Eltham station-New Addington), replacing MetroRiders, a type now longer in the fleet.

The remaining full-sized single-deckers are LV1-12 dual-doored, Plaxton-bodied Dennis Lances, new ear in 1994. These can now be found working from Bromley garage on route 227 (Bromley North station-Crystal Palace), formerly operated by Kentish Bus.

The last MetroRiders were ousted by the MB class c Mercedes-Benz Varios with Plaxton Beaver 29-seat bodies. They are allocated to Plumstead and Catford garages.

Above: *Leyland Olympians also feature in the fleet, with over 60 on the books. ECW-bodied L131 (D131 FYM) is caught in traffic in Rushey Green, Catford after an April shower while on route 185 (Lewisham-Victoria).* **Kevin Lane**

Right: *In an unusual move, Selkent and Metrobus took over joint operation of central London route C1 in February 1998, given up by London General due to staff shortages. This was however, only until the June, pending its planned takeover by a new operator to the capital, Travel London. Selkent used Mercedes-Benz Varios, including MB3 (R503 YWC) holding up traffic for a moment in Buckingham Palace Road, Victoria, early in March 1998.* **Kevin Lane**

ellings-Golden Miller Ltd

A Wintersells Road, Byfleet, Surrey, KT14 7LF

lings-Golden Miller, formed from the amalgamation
Tellings Coaches, Byfleet, and Golden Miller,
itham, took on its first LT contracts in August 1991
'h routes 116 and 117 won from Westlink, although
ese passed to London & Country (then an
sociated company) after less than a year's
eration. However, route S3 (Worcester Park station-
tton Hospital) was awarded and commenced
eration in April 1995 and a second route, 235
entford-Sunbury Village), was won from London
ited and began in January 1998. A number of other
ites are run under contract to Surrey County
uncil and a coaching fleet is also available for
vate hire etc.

Mini and midibuses are prominent in the fleet, which
is mainly Mercedes-Benz but includes a pair of Optare
StarRiders that originated with London Buses. The
235 route demands Dennis Darts, 14 Plaxton Pointer
SLFs being used on this service. Buses are blue,
yellow and white.

*Below: The operation of former London United route
235 (Brentford-Sunbury Village) was assumed from
January 1998, 14 Plaxton Pointer-bodied Dennis Dart
SLFs being acquired for the service. R506 SJM
passes through Hounslow in March 1998.*
Kevin Lane

*Left: A pair of Optare
StarRiders, new to London
Buses but acquired from a
Scottish operator, entered the
fleet in December 1997. F34
CWY, formerly SR34, is
pictured in Sutton on route S3
(Worcester Park Station-
Sutton Hospital) in March
1998.* **Kevin Lane**

87

Above: Surrey County Council route 511 runs from Esher to Kingston Hospital. Tellings-Golden Miller P702 LCF, one of six Mercedes-Benz Varios with Plaxton Beaver bodies bought in 1997, passes through Kingston in March 1998. **Kevin Lane**

Thamesway

Stapleford Close, New Writtle Street, Chelmsford, Essex, CM2 0SD

Thamesway was formed from the division of former NBC subsidiary Eastern National in July 1990, by then owned by Badgerline Holdings. This company was responsible for those routes in London and South Essex, operations previously marketed as Eastern National Citybus. Eastern National and Thamesway were reunited as Essex Buses, now part of FirstGroup, from 1996, although separate fleetnames were retained.

Eastern National was there at the beginning of London Transport tendering in July 1985, successfully bidding for routes 193 and W9, two routes still operated under Thamesway. During the intervening years, a number of routes have been won, retained or lost, although some 12 tendered routes are currently operated, together with some 10 mobility routes in east London. This is in addition to other routes in Essex.

Routes 193, 362, 379, 389, 399, 462, D8, W9, W11-13 are in the hands of Mercedes midibuses, leaving just the 191 with Dennis Darts. The mobility routes require three more Darts: Marshall-bodied 17-seaters.

All routes, with the exception of the 193 and the mobility routes, are operated from the depot in Ponders End, the others from Basildon. The current Thamesway livery is yellow and maroon, although the mobility buses are red.

Right: Thamesway have four Marshall-bodied Dennis Darts available for mobility routes, 851-54. No 853 (N853 CPU) was operating in Romford in February 1998. **Kevin Lane**

ove: Mercedes-Benz 709D/Reeve Burgess Beaver 246 (F246 MVW) leaves Walthamstow on a W11 to *ingford Hall Estate in November 1996.* **Kevin Lane**

F. E. Thorpe

272 Latimer Road, North Kensington, London W10 6QY

Frank E. Thorpe & Son operates mainly mobility routes, including perhaps the most well known, Stationlink SL1/SL2, connecting the various termini.

Both begin at Paddington, SL1 running towards Marylebone, the SL2 towards Victoria. This service was formerly known as Stationlink (and Carelink

fore that) on which London General had introduced tare City Pacers, which ran in a distinctive red and low livery. F. E. Thorpe has operated the service ce October 1992 and currently uses Optare Excels, gistered N100/N200/N300/N400 FET, seating 27 d of course featuring wheelchair lifts. These nicles run in a red and yellow livery also.

April 1995 saw the start of route C4 (Putney Pier-Hurlingham) on which MCW MetroRiders are employed. Further LT work was gained from August 1997, with the acquisition of the mobility routes of Javelin Coaches, Wandsworth, while the 210 (Brent Cross-Finsbury Park station) is due to be transferred from Grey-Green later in 1998.

*ft: Four Optare Excels are in the fleet for Stationlink routes SL1/2; N200 FET is seen at London Bridge station February 1998. **Kevin Lane***

low left: Among the vehicles taken over from Javelin Coaches in 1997 was this Wadham Stringer-bodied ercedes-Benz 709D, J520 WTW. It was pictured off-service at Paddington station in April 1998. vin Lane

Sightseeing and Other Buses

e buses running LT services are not the whole ry, however. In central London, sightseeing buses e well in evidence, open-top in the summer and metimes closed-top during the winter months. veral operators are currently prominent in this field, luding London Coaches, London Pride and The Big s Company. Information on the various tours offered n be found in leaflets obtainable at stations and urist information centres.

ondon Coaches now concentrates on sightseeing rk, following the setting up of London Coaches nt), trading as North Kent Express, to deal with the mmuter side of the business. The sightseeing erations of another operator, Blue Triangle, were quired in March 1997, with Arriva plc taking over e whole London Coaches operation in December 97. Hopefully, the red and cream fleet will not ccumb to turquoise and cream! Buses are branded 'The Original London Sightseeing Tour'.

he London Coaches fleet consists of around 80 hicles — a mixture of Routemasters, Metrobuses, stol VRs and a few odd Metroliners and Daimler etlines.

ondon Pride, previously owned by EnsignBus, was d in February 1998 to a group who formerly ran the ndon Coaches sightseeing operations. Metrobuses d Dennis Dominators are in favour at the moment ether with a number of Metroliners, the largest uble-deckers in London. Other odds and ends lude a few Leyland Titans, of both TNLX and PD3 es, and a pair of ex-London RTs. Buses are red and ver, carrying the slogan 'This is an Official London htseeing Bus'.

he maroon and cream buses of The Big Bus mpany run on three routes: red, blue and green.

Former London Titans are currently replacing DMS-type Daimler and Leyland Fleetlines, the latter once regarded as the standard London sightseeing bus. However, perhaps its most well-known bus is ex-East Kent Road Car AEC Regent VPFN 853, a likeness of which appears in its publicity. Three Routemasters are among other vehicles in stock.

Stage carriage services of other operators may be encountered on the edge of the London area, sometimes penetrating further under agreement with London Transport. Large towns just inside the LT area are logical terminal points. Romford, for example, sees Blue Triangle's route 265 from Bulphan as well as Eastern National into Essex. Also from Essex, as well as Hertfordshire, come other Arriva East Herts & Essex routes, including the 505 which makes it as far as Walthamstow from Harlow. To the south of London, the various Kent and Surrey Arriva companies are all regular operators into Kent and Surrey, to centres such as Bromley, Croydon and Kingston.

At Heathrow Airport, Speedlink undertakes various shuttle and other contract work, which includes 26 Wright-bodied Volvo B6LEs finished in a dark blue livery for 'Heathrow Hotel Hoppa' services. Nineteen DAF SB220/Plaxton Prestige low-floor single-deckers are currently being used to link the airport with a temporary station at Stockley Park, near Hayes. From here the Fast Train service to Paddington terminates pending the completion of the rail-link into the airport during summer 1998. To the west of the airport is the village of Poyle, terminus of Ashford Luxury Coaches' route 305 from Staines. Used on this service is H754 DTM, a Reeve Burgess-bodied Mercedes-Benz 811D. New in 1990, it was acquired from Armchair in 1996, replacing a former National Car Parks Leyland

National 2. Also in the area is Metro Travel's route M1, running four times on Saturdays only between Watford Junction and Staines, using a Leyland National.

Uxbridge is another 'border town', with the Arriva the Shires and Beeline in evidence on local services. Seamarks of Luton reach Mount Vernon Hospital, just inside the LT boundary, on route R2 from Rickmansworth. Lastly, another operator to note is Universitybus, whose 614 from Hatfield reaches Edgware and Harrow, Mondays to Fridays.

A number of other operators may be seen on express and limited-stop services in London. Arriva Kent & Sussex, Sovereign and Arriva the Shires for instance work under the Green Line name, while heading into Aldgate and beyond, can be seen Arriva Southend double-deckers and coaches. Arriva East Herts & Essex route 724 links Harlow with Heathrow,

the recipient of new DAF SB220 dual-purpose vehicles, while coaches from the Leaside Travel fleet may be seen on the 711 Harlow to Victoria. Grey-Green also works commuter services in from Essex. Two operators from Oxford are Oxford Citylink and Stagecoach's Oxford Tube. The BeeLine runs a number of services into London and to Heathrow from Berkshire. From the Reading area, Reading Transport operates in on several routes under the 'London Line'. United Counties, another Stagecoach company, also works in from the Bedford and Kettering areas. North Kent Express vehicles are also much in evidence on commuter workings to and from North Kent. As mentioned in the 'Where to Go' section of this book, National Express workings converge on Victoria Coach Station.

Left: London Pride 401 (B121 ORU) is 1984 MCW Metroliner seating 83, 63 of those on the top deck, reason enough for their popularity on sightseeing work in London. The bus, acquired from Midland Red North in 1990, is seen crawling along Embankment. **Kevin Lane**

Right: The former London Coaches operations from Wandsworth are now under Arriva ownership. RM307 (WLT 307) drums up business at Trafalgar Square on a dull March morning in 1998. Note the nearside doors to allow wheelchair access via a lift. **Kevin Lane**

Left: Some limited-stop services into London use double-deck vehicles, including Arriva Southend Volvo Olympian/Northern Counties N708 TPK heads for home along Commercial Road, Limehouse in February 1998. **Kevin Lane**

Right: Some National Express workings to and from the north seem to call at Golders Green. Heading into London on service 561 in January 1998 is K526 RJX, a Van Hool-bodied DAF SB3000 of AJC Coaches, Leeds. It was new in 1993 and acquired from Hallmark, Luton two years later. **Kevin Lane**

Left: Towns on the edge of the London area will see a mix of London and provincial buses. More interesting than many is this Universitybus National Greenway, originally London Buses LS261 (THX 261S). It is leaving Edgware in October 1997 working back to Hatfield from Queensbury. **Kevin Lane**

Appendix 1:
Class Prefixes;
Former London Bus Companies

Class prefix letters to fleetnumbers have been a feature of London buses since London General introduced them from 1909. Following privatisation, the new companies have tended to continue with this system, although there has been the odd lapse; Selkent, for example, have not given prefixes to their Northern Counties-bodied Volvo Olympians nor to Alexander-bodied Dennis Darts. Whether the use of class prefixes will be perpetuated in the future is open to speculation, although I suspect that the Arriva Group may be an early contender to renumber their

London fleets into a common series. The list that follows reveals several occasions where the same class prefix will denote a different type of vehicle to another company, or that similarly, the same type of vehicle will receive a different prefix. For example, an Alexander-bodied Volvo Olympian with East London or Westlink is classified VA, whereas with London Central and Metroline they are AV. To confuse matters further, a VA with Arriva North London is an Alexander-bodied Volvo Citybus.

Double-deck types:

A	Volvo Olympian/Alexander Royale
AV	Volvo Olympian/Alexander RH
AV	Volvo Olympian/Alexander Royale
DBS	DAF/Northern Counties Palatine II
DRM	Routemaster with platform doors
L	Leyland Olympian/Alexander
L	Leyland Olympian/ECW
L	Leyland Olympian/Leyland
L	Leyland Olympian/Northern Counties
LA	Leyland Olympian/Alexander
LN	Leyland Olympian/Northern Counties
M	MCW Metrobus
NV	Volvo Olympian/Northern Counties Palatine I/II
RM	Routemaster
RMC	Routemaster Coach
RML	Routemaster Lengthened
S	Scania/Alexander
RHS	Scania/Northern Counties Palatine I
SP	DAF/Optare Spectra
T	Leyland Titan
V	Volvo Olympian/Northern Counties Palatine II
VA	Volvo Citybus/Alexander
VA	Volvo Olympian/Alexander RH
VA	Volvo Olympian/Alexander RL
VC	Volvo Citybus/Northern Counties
VE	Volvo Citybus/East Lancs
VN	Volvo Olympian/Northern Counties Palatine I

Single-deck types (excluding Dennis Darts):

BL	Bristol LH/ECW
DA	DAF/Optare Delta
DAF	DAF/Ikarus Citibus
DAF	DAF/Optare Delta
DIB	DAF/Ikarus Citibus
DLP	DAF/Plaxton Prestige
GLS	Leyland National Greenway
LLW	Dennis Lance/Wright Pathfinder
LN	Dennis Lance/Northern Counties Paladin
LS	Leyland National
LV	Dennis Lance/Plaxton Verde
LX	Leyland Lynx
MM	MAN/Marshall
MV	MAN/Optare Vecta
RF	AEC Regal IV
SLW	Scania/Wright Pathfinder
VWL	Volvo B6/Wright Crusader
XL	Optare XL

Dennis Darts:

CD	Dennis Dart SLF/Wright Crusader (10.2m)
D	Dennis Dart/Plaxton Pointer (9.8m)
DAL	Dennis Dart/Alexander Dash (9.8m)
DC	Dennis Dart/Duple or Carlyle Dartline (9.0m)
DEL	Dennis Dart/East Lancs (9.0m)
DL	Dennis Dart SLF/Plaxton Pointer (10.0m)
DLD	Dennis Dart SLF/Plaxton Pointer (10.0m dual-door)
DLP	Dennis Dart SLF/Plaxton Pointer (9.2m)

LS	Dennis Dart SLF/Plaxton Pointer (9.2m)		LDP	Dennis Dart SLF/Plaxton Pointer (9.2m)
M	Dennis Dart SLF/Marshall Capital (9.4m)		LDP	Dennis Dart SLF/Plaxton Pointer (10.0m)
M	Dennis Dart/Marshall (9.8m)		LDR	Dennis Dart/Plaxton Pointer (9.8m)
ML	Dennis Dart SLF/Marshall (10.2m)		PD	Dennis Dart/Plaxton Pointer(9.8m)
MS	Dennis Dart SLF/Marshall (9.4m)		SLD	Dennis Dart SLF/Alexander
NL	Dennis Dart/Northern Counties			ALX200 (10.2m)
	Paladin (9.0m)			

P	Dennis Dart/Plaxton Pointer (9.0m)
P	Dennis Dart/Plaxton Pointer (9.8m)
PL	Dennis Dart/Plaxton Pointer (9.0m)
R	Dennis Dart/Plaxton Pointer (8.5m)
R	Dennis Dart/Reeves Burgess
	Pointer (8.5m)
RL	Dennis Dart/Plaxton Pointer (9.0m)
T	Dennis Dart/Carlyle Dartline (8.5m)
T	Dennis Dart/Duple Dartline (8.5m)
W	Dennis Dart/Wright (8.5m)
WL	Dennis Dart/Wright Handybus (9.0m)
DR	Dennis Dart/Plaxton Pointer (9.8m)
	Dennis Dart SLF/Plaxton Pointer (10.0m)
CY	Dennis Dart SLF/Alexander
	ALX200 (10.25m)

Mini and Midibuses:

LC	LDV400/Crystals
MA	Mercedes-Benz 811D/Alexander
ML	Marshall Minibus
MM	Mercedes-Benz/Marshall
MR	MCW MetroRider MF150
MRL	MCW MetroRider MF158
MRL	Optare MetroRider
MT	Mercedes-Benz 709D/
	Reeve Burgess Beaver
MW	Mercedes-Benz 811D/Wright Nimbus
RW	Renault-Dodge S75/Wright
SC	Freight Rover Sherpa/Carlyle Citibus
SR	Mercedes-Benz 811D/Optare StarRider

Appendix 2:
The Major Bus-Owning Groups in London

ARRIVA
Arriva Croydon & North Surrey Ltd
(formerly London & Country and Londonlinks)
Arriva East Herts & Essex Ltd
(formerly County Bus & Coach)
Arriva Kent Thamesside Ltd
(formerly Kentish Bus & Coach)
Arriva London North Ltd (formerly Leaside Buses)
Arriva London North-East Ltd (formerly Grey-Green)
Arriva London South Ltd (formerly South London)
Arriva The Shires Ltd (formerly LDT the Shires)
Arriva also now own the London Coaches
sightseeing operations.

2. BLAZEFIELD HOLDINGS
London Sovereign and Sovereign Harrow.

3. FIRSTGROUP
CentreWest, London Buslines and Thamesway.

4. GO-AHEAD
London Central and London General.

5. MTL TRUST HOLDINGS
MTL London.

6. STAGECOACH HOLDINGS
East London and Selkent.

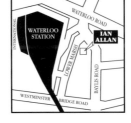